Happy Mondays

Create a Company Culture in which People
Love to Go to Work!

Kristin E. Robertson

Brio Leadership Press
Colleyville, TX

PRAISE FOR HAPPY MONDAYS

"How do you grow a positive, vibrant company culture? You embed core values in everything that you do as a company. Robertson has done a fantastic job of defining the working parts of a values-based business. We've learned many good tips from working with Kristin Robertson. Follow her prescriptions, and you can grow your own unique and sustainable business. Remember, as Peter Drucker famously said, 'Culture eats strategy for lunch!'"

—Tom Niesen, CEO, Acuity Systems

"Culture is shaped by everything you do. Align all your processes and leadership to the values and purpose of your company. Leaders set the tone for the company, so if you change the way leaders lead, you change the culture. The examples I've tried to set as CEO of our company, and the values-driven leadership development that Kristin Robertson has provided us are some of the reasons we've been one of the most successful distributorships in our industry."

—Carol Roehrig, CEO, BKM Total Office of Texas

"A strong culture is critical to long-term business success and this book will give you the framework to build and enhance your culture, including practical ideas and inspirational stories. The company rituals and routines that we've put in place have shaped who we are and reinforced the values our culture is built on, and this book has given us even more ideas to explore!"

—Tina Young, CEO, Marketwave

"Culture must be built intentionally. As Kristin Robertson says, there are only two kinds of culture: an intentional one and an unintentional one. Don't let the tail-wag-the-dog: mold your culture to the positive values YOU wish to demonstrate to the world. We learned this the hard way, by trial and error. Now you can read this book, follow Robertson's suggestions, and create your own Company Culture Ecosystem that disrupts your industry and transforms the lives of your team members, clients and community. Read this book!"

—Steven Neuner, CEO, Alkali Insurance

"Purpose and values have been the bedrock of our company from the first day I started it. It's been an honor to work with Kristin Robertson to further the ideals of a purpose-driven company. This book provides you the framework to grow a positive, values-based company culture. We are beginning to use many of her ideas at our company to positive results. I want to grow a company where everyone, including myself, enjoys coming to work. Values-based work environments are the only sustainable ecosystem!"

—Terri Maxwell, CEO, Share on Purpose

Library of Congress Cataloguing-in-Publication data
Library of Congress Control Number: 2016918609

Happy Mondays: Create a Company Culture in which People Love to Go to Work!

Kristin E. Robertson—2nd ed.

Brio Leadership Press

ISBN-10:   0-9823414-3-1
ISBN-13:   978-0-9823414-3-8

Contents

Dedicated to Adam, my dear husband, who has been a loyal companion and supporter in all my many endeavors. I trust you have never been bored.

Preface

Wouldn't you like to have Happy Mondays in your organization? A positive, productive and performance-enhancing culture can ensure that your team members are excited to come to work every day, especially Mondays.

In my consulting and leadership coaching work, too often I hear sad stories of people who are *not* happy to go to work. One client said she got stomachaches every Sunday night as she contemplated going to her job in a toxic organization. Another told me he would often wish to have a small accident on his commute to work so he had an excuse not to go into the office.

What a waste of human potential this is! My deepest wish is that this book can help create more positive company cultures, where people thrive, are valued and held accountable.

My fascination with company culture began early in my career, as I experienced both the worst and the best of company cultures in just a few years. I was working as a client support analyst for a software company that seemed to have no respect for its employees or clients, given how poorly both constituencies were treated. I was supporting accounting software that was released before it was free of mission-critical bugs, and even though the program simply didn't work as promised, I was expected to make customers happy.

I dreaded going to work on Mondays and was unhappy with my career progress. There was no place to go in this sad company. I did what any sane person would do—I looked for another job.

When I confided about my job search to a trusted colleague, she recommended that I apply at her husband's start-up company. I protested, saying that I wasn't interested in a new, risky company.

"But this company is different, Kristin," she insisted.

After several interviews with both founders of the company, I agreed with her and accepted the job. What ensued were the best years of my professional career, a time of rapid learning, growth, and high achievement for both me and the company. I was promoted within a few years to Vice President of Client Services, where I was instrumental in building a culture of customer service, achievement, accountability, excellence and fun. Having experienced the personal fulfillment and heady excitement of working in that environment, my experience as an executive and consultant at subsequent companies often paled in comparison.

Those formative years of my career shaped my purpose and passion into my current roles of entrepreneur, consultant, speaker, and executive coach. My moniker is "The Happy Mondays Coach" and our team's purpose statement is to "ensure your employees are excited to go to work on Monday morning." I have personally experienced both dread and excitement on Monday mornings in various companies, at various times of my life, and in various roles, so I know the impact of both states of mind.

Engaged employees—those people who are happy to be there and are fulfilled by their work—are more productive, creative, and loyal. It is in a company's best interest to build great cultures that create engaged employees.

This book is a must-have for any leader who wishes to grow a sustainable and flourishing company culture. The first section includes introductory information on what culture is and isn't. After this, I introduce a model for conceptualizing the salient elements of your culture, called the *Company Culture Ecosystem*. This is a framework for designing your culture: you will want to pay attention to all the elements of the *Company Culture Ecosystem*, and exactly how you decide to do each element will be unique to your company. This ecosystem is also unique in the literature on company culture in that it includes operational and accountability concerns, both of which are vital in developing a vibrant, results-oriented company culture.

Then we'll examine each element of the *Company Culture Ecosystem* in depth.

Interspersed between chapters are case studies of companies that I've observed and researched. Each company's case study highlights some aspect of their culture that is particularly noteworthy.

You'll also find several sidebar conversations about pertinent elements of culture, like creating vision boards at the beginning of the year. At the end of each chapter is a summary of key points—a checklist, if you will, of the important points to remember.

Are you ready to experience Happy Mondays?

OK, let's get started.

Kristin E. Robertson
Colleyville, TX
June 2019

"Culture eats strategy for lunch."

—Peter Drucker

CHAPTER 1

Company Culture: Is It Important?

Steven Neuner started Alkali Benefits and Insurance Services (Alkali) from his home in 2005. At first, it was just he and his wife making calls to friends and family to sell them insurance. Alkali was started in the extra bedroom of the Neuner house.

Steven freely admits that he was naïve about company culture, with no awareness of the importance of establishing a positive company culture, let alone how to build and sustain it. He had an idea of what he wanted to do, based on previous jobs. In the beginning, Steven and his business partner/wife Corey made a lot of hiring mistakes: they hired people who had knowledge and experience in the insurance field. Many people left after only a few months, were disruptive and didn't get along with the team, or didn't produce expected results. They simply didn't understand what Steven was trying to do, which was to massively disrupt the insurance brokerage business with his innovative methods.

Learning through the school of hard knocks, Steven and Corey started thinking about their culture, what they stood for at Alkali Insurance, and the impact they wanted to make on their clients, their team members, and their community.

Eventually, they created the Alkali Ten Best Habits, incorporating their values into behavioral descriptions. They started hiring to these "Habits" by creating a preliminary phone interview structure that asked open-ended questions pertaining to each of the "Habits" and the candidate's past behaviors in those areas. They used a ten-question interview form to ask about their culture fit, like self-awareness. They created values-embedding rituals like the knighting ceremony, in which leaders hosted new hires at a medieval-themed dinner theatre at the completion of their initial training. Once the new hires are knighted (yes, they bow and get tapped on the shoulder with a fake sword), each person signs the pledge, which lists the guiding principles and behaviors of the company which hangs in the office reception area. With the help of their best team members, the company created a new hire training program, refining it over time, based on feedback and results from their training classes.

To systemize the business, the leadership team created a unique trademarked process called The Empowered Advantage™ that defines a standard of exemplary client care, setting and sets them apart from other insurance brokers. They designed a schedule of regular meetings that incorporated these traditions and rituals. The leadership team designed a system of monitoring team members' phone calls and reviewing their results and establishing a rhythm of monthly coaching based on positive feedback from each team member. They started a "no gossip and slander policy," which eliminates backstabbing in the workplace. In the team member handbook, they established a zero-tolerance attitude toward gossip and mean-spirited communication, stating that non-compliance can lead to disciplinary measures, up to and including termination of employment. Instead, team members are encouraged to address concerns directly with the targeted person.

The result of these combined efforts and practices? Ten years of increasing financial results, the longer tenure of good team members, sky high client retention rates, and the distinct possibility of revolutionizing the insurance industry market for the better.

Steven hopes that other companies learn from his mistakes. His advice: don't delay defining core values and culture until you have turnover issues. Instead, define what you stand for in the early days of establishing your company, so you can build culture from the ground up. In other words, do it right the first time. Steven has the same advice for larger companies and established departments: define your desired culture and start working it without delay.

What Is Culture?

It's an old joke that bears repeating in the context of company culture: A grandmother fish swims by two youngster fishes and casually remarks,

"The water sure is nice today, isn't it?"

Confused, the youngsters look at each other and say, "What water?"

Organizational culture is like the water in which fish swim or the air that humans breathe; we are surrounded by, live in, and depend on it but, until someone points it out to us, we are unaware of exactly what it is. This makes it imperative to start this book with a definition of culture. When human beings form organizations, a culture naturally develops. People in groups intuitively form unspoken rules about what is OK and not OK to say, do and behave toward each other, usually based on the example that leaders set. Organizations can have one of two types of cultures: an intentional or unintentional one. Only when leaders intentionally take responsibility for building, exemplifying, and sustaining a culture does it become a positive, vibrant one.

> **Organizations can have one of two cultures: intentional or unintentional.**

4

So, what exactly is company culture? Here's our definition: culture is made up of the values, underlying beliefs, and behavioral norms found in each organization. Behavioral norms are the unspoken rules that govern acceptable behaviors ways of acting in the company. For example, a behavioral norm at a company could be that everyone addresses managers as "Mr. So-and-So" or "Ms. So-and-So" and everyone else is referred to by their first name. An example of a company belief is: "We are the elite team. We are good—really good."

Edgar Schein, the leading academic authority on culture (2010, 14), has equated a corporate culture to an individual's personality; in other words, culture is to an organization as personality is to an individual. Culture is an abstraction that can only be seen through its manifestations, such as employee retention, productivity, and profitability.

With the growing attention paid to the importance of culture in the last two decades, it seems that everything has been dumped into the culture bucket. It's therefore important to make a distinction between culture and climate, which are different aspects of an organization's interpersonal structure.

Climate is concerned with the attitudes, perceptions and feelings toward situations encountered in the organization. Climate, therefore, is an artifact or manifestation of culture; it is a subset of culture. Unlike culture, climate is easy to measure and by far, easier to change. Employee satisfaction and engagement surveys are examples of climate instruments, and they can be swayed by recent situations. For example, if a company

There is no one-size-fits-all perfect culture.

just announced a change in benefits that is favorable to employees, the climate of the organization would improve. However, the glow or good feelings from that announcement will fade over time while the culture of the organization will endure unchanged.

Although it is harder to measure and difficult to change, culture is important and can help a company achieve its goals through its climate-related manifestations, one of which is employee engagement (Sisodia et al. 2014). As Peter Drucker famously quipped, "Culture eats strategy for lunch" (Mackey et al. 2014), meaning that it takes an engaged workforce to implement an excellent strategy.

Culture is the result of everything you do in a company; how you treat employees, customers, and vendors; how you design your operational processes; how you set standards of performance and hold people accountable to them.

This book answers the following questions:

- What is the culture of a company, and why is it important?

- How can a leader embed the desired culture into either a rapidly growing organization, or one that is well-established but in need of a cultural reboot?

- What are the tools needed to shape or reshape a culture?

This book will guide you through the process of growing a sustainable business in a throwaway world, using the *Company Culture Ecosystem* as a model. Every company has a culture whether it is intentional or not, so why not grow a flourishing culture intentionally, by making everything you do a reflection of the culture that you desire?

In companies both large and small, it takes continual reinforcement to sustain and uphold strong, positive cultural values, which are the foundation of a strong culture.

Growing an organizational culture is not a one-and-done activity; rather, it is built over time and must be carefully and continuously nurtured by leaders.

Does Company Culture Make a Difference?

Schein observes that the "goodness" of a culture depends on the culture's relationship to the environment in which the company operates (2010, 14). In other words, there is no one-size-fits-all perfect culture for all organizations. What may work well for one company in a certain industry, operating in a certain region of the world, with its unique leadership style, may not suit another company with different characteristics.

Think of Apple and Microsoft—both companies are in high technology but have vastly different cultures that were largely built on the values and personalities of their founders. Therefore, prescriptions of *how* to create a perfect culture are misleading. Rather, consider *what* you need to include in designing a positive culture, and, yes, gather ideas from other organizations, but define your own culture.

This advice is particularly pertinent to the values you and your organization choose to honor. **Several longitudinal studies provide impressive metrics to show that strong cultures contribute to financial success.** The core values that one company holds dear may not be relevant to a company in a different environment.

Many studies have proven that a strong, positive enterprise culture produces beneficial financial results. Even those researchers who cannot bring themselves to proclaim culture as the key to success nevertheless admit that it matters (Trice and Beyer 1984, 21; Keyton 2011, 73).

More importantly, several longitudinal studies provide impressive metrics to show that strong cultures contribute to financial success (Sisodia et al. 2014; Collins 2001; Kotter and Heskett 1992; Mackey et al. 2014; Rhoades et al. 2011). Raj Sisodia, professor of marketing at Babson University and a founder of the Conscious Capitalism movement, along with his team studied companies that they designated as "firms of endearment (2014)."

"Firms of endearment" are companies that actively align all stakeholders' interests and consider corporate culture their most important asset (2014, 8–11). They report that the public companies on their firms of endearment list returned "1,026 percent for investors over the 10 years ending June 30, 2006, compared to 122 percent for the S&P 500, that's more than an 8-to-1 ratio!" (2014, 16)

In another study, Harvard Business School professors John Kotter and James Heskett conducted an eleven-year study of 207 companies and concluded those with cultures that focus on the key constituencies of customers, stockholders, and employees outperformed their competition by large margins (1992, 11).

A 2008 American Management Association study equates a "positive corporate culture" with higher performance (Rhoades 2011, 2). Denison (1984) finds that a "participative culture" has measurable effects on a company's performance. He used two financial measures, Return on Sales and Return on Investment, to compare results among companies that he rated along the dimensions of cultural characteristics, management practices, and key precepts. Sørensen's research (2002) finds that companies with strong, that is, consistent cultures perform better than their peers during stable market environments, but the benefits disappear in volatile environments.

Some experts use indirect measures of a good company culture to prove benefits. Some indirect measures are employee engagement or satisfaction and ethical business practices. For example, the companies on Fortune's "100 Best Companies to Work For" list (a measure of employee satisfaction and engagement) post stock-market returns that beat their peers by 2-3% per year (Backman 2014).

One can also examine ethical measures as an indirect indicator for good cultures. Per Mitchell & Ethisphere, ethical companies outperformed the S&P 500 every year since 2007 by 7.3 percent. (Mackey, et al. 2014, 280)

However, several issues remain in proving that company culture positively impacts financial success. Wilderom, Glunk, and Maslowski (as cited in Schein 2010, 14) list two such issues as: (1) the variety of definitions of what is a "good" company culture and (2) the variety of different performance indices used to measure culture. As noted above, the authors who report superior financial performance of companies with outstanding cultures use different measurements of good culture.

However, only during markets where unemployment is low and employees have a choice of jobs does treating employees well contribute to financial success. The US is currently in such a market. At the time of this book's publication, the US Bureau of Labor Statistics reports a relatively low unemployment rate of 3.6 percent. Conversely, if the economy is poor, unemployment is high, and workers do not have choice in where they work, there is little economic incentive to treat employees well.

The characterization of culture as the norms, values, and beliefs of a company is a good starting point, but unsatisfactory in that it seems too academic. How do we put our arms around organizational culture and define it in ways that make practical, down-to-earth sense? Those questions bring us to the next chapter, in which we will introduce the *Company Culture Ecosystem*.

Key Concepts

1. Culture is the set of values, expected behaviors, underlying beliefs and norms found in each organization.

2. Culture is like a company's personality. Just like individual personality types, there is no one best culture.

3. Company culture is built and sustained over time. To grow a flourishing ecosystem, the culture must be tended daily.

4. Several studies show that growing a vibrant culture can result in higher employee retention and engagement, improved productivity and increased profits.

CHAPTER 2

The Company Culture Ecosystem

Business models are useful because they provide a framework for thinking about an issue or attacking a problem. Models are like a 3-D mobile of the solar system—they are a construct or analytical system that points to reality. In business, models help leaders conceptualize and organize the many competing priorities needed to run a business.

Here, we introduce the Company Culture Ecosystem model, which combines several academic models of organizational culture into a practical, feet-on-the-ground framework for examining it. The *Company Culture Ecosystem* serves as a checklist for designing and sustaining organizational culture.

The *Company Culture Ecosystem* includes the six interdependent and necessary components of a vibrant work culture. These aspects of organizational life depict the cultural causal factors, or the levers to push to affect change in the culture. When all elements are in alignment, the culture (and therefore the company) functions well. When an element or two are missing or are weak, the company does not perform optimally.

To provide an overview, the following introduces each element of the *Company Culture Ecosystem*. Subsequent chapters will provide in-depth explanations of and how-to instructions for each element.

The Company Culture Ecosystem

Values and Purpose

The core values are the ideals that the company wishes to honor in its corporate life.

Many business leaders think limited resources of time and money constrain their ability to create meaningful rituals and events to support, maintain, and celebrate the organization's espoused values. They scoff at other company's extravagant practices, saying that those organizations have big pockets and can afford lavish rituals and boondoggles.

Often, this means that sustaining the espoused values is left to chance, typically resulting in the toleration of behaviors and norms that run counter to the organization's declared values.

It is not sufficient to educate employees once about cultural values and norms; rather, the espoused values of an organization must be nurtured in the daily life of the company, including the decision-making, people practices, operational processes, and customer-service standards.

A purpose statement describes the greater good results the organization wishes to achieve. All companies can identify a purpose to their efforts besides enriching the bank accounts of their owners.

Wise leaders will uncover that purpose and use it to inspire employees, customers and suppliers. A motivating purpose sustains the *Company Culture Ecosystem*.

Leadership

Culture is set by the leaders of the company. Schein states that if leaders do not actively manage the culture, "the culture will manage them" (22). Another phrase that reflects the oversized influence of leaders on the culture is what is called the "Tone at the Top." As we know from emotional intelligence studies, leaders set the emotional climate of an organization, are the role models for expected behavior, and thus enforce or detract from organizational values. Developing the emotional intelligence characteristics of self-awareness, humility, empathy, compassion, accountability, and trust is the best way for a leader to affect a positive culture.

People Practices

We've already established that culture is the sum of how you treat people: employees, customers, suppliers, and

Leaders set the emotional climate of an organization and are the role models for expected behavior.

the community. The good news is that how management treats employees is the predictor for how all other constituencies are treated. How you interact with your team members will be reflected in how they treat customers and suppliers. And the level of care shown to your employees will be reflected in how your company cares for the community. It is all one fabric.

Rituals, Symbols, and Stories

It is not enough to develop core values, print them out, and post them on a bulletin board. Values, assumptions, and beliefs are taught to team members by leaders who model them and are best taught in a repetitive manner to keep them top of mind. Drip-irrigation, rather than a flood followed by drought, is the best way to nourish both a garden and a company culture.

Examples of routines/rituals include how you schedule and organize meetings, what rituals are repeated at each one, how you routinely celebrate success, and the regularly scheduled social gatherings you provide employees.

I once made a sales call at the corporate headquarters of Medtronic, the medical device company located in Minneapolis, Minnesota. As I sat down in the reception area to wait for my sales prospect, I noticed a beautiful book, called *The Medtronic Way*, on the coffee table. I opened it and was mesmerized by the story of Medtronic's history, founders, and timeline of innovative devices it released to the market. The book was full of photos—of employees, customers, and patients—and commentary on the life of the company.

This is what I mean by stories—the stories you tell about your company. Choose the positive ones to repeat within your company.

Be intentional about the methods used to get work done and the tools you provide to do so.

Symbols are the tangibles that you see in your office, starting with the branding of the company and extending to the type of furnishings in the office. Is there a Persian rug, or a second-hand conference table in the conference room? Each of these symbolizes the personality of the company.

Operational Processes and Tools

Because your culture is embedded in everything you do, whether you are aware of it or not, it is important to be intentional about the methods used to get work done and the tools you provide to do so. Core values can be consciously included in your operational procedures, and the tools that you provide your employees will be emblematic of the culture.

For instance, if you provide outdated computers to the least paid workers in your company, that will represent a hierarchical value system in the company.

In contrast, if you provide everyone updated computers on the same refresh schedule, you will demonstrate a culture in which everyone is appreciated.

Accountability Systems

This element includes all the ways that employees are held accountable, starting with strategic goals and cascading through departmental objectives and, ultimately, into individual goals and plans. It encompasses the metrics used to measure the progress and success of everyone in the organization and the company itself.

This element is vital to culture. Without it, culture is simply an intangible, feel-good abstraction. With accountability systems come manageability, trust, safety, and security.

Key Concepts

1. Like an ecosystem, a company's culture is made up of many interdependent elements. *The Company Culture Ecosystem* model identifies six elements that must be in alignment: Values and Purpose; Leadership;

People Practices; Rituals, Symbols and Stories; Operational Processes; and Accountability Systems.

2. Of the six elements of *The Company Culture Ecosystem*, values and purpose are the foundation of your company's culture, but leadership quality is the most powerful fertilizer of a flourishing culture. For that reason, the leadership chapter of this book is the longest.

3. All six elements must be designed to uphold the core values of the company.

4. All six elements must be strong and working together to grow a vibrant company culture.

CHAPTER 3

The Cultural Transformation Process

A cultural transformation, whether for a start-up organization or a well-established one, must start from the top. The top official must be visibly and emotionally involved in this kind of change effort. Unless team members view and understand the seriousness with which the chief executive approaches this project, the effort will not produce the desired results. Not only that, but the entire leadership team must be visibly supportive of the transformation. Leaders set the example and the emotional mood of an organization; if they scoff at an innovation, the rest of their team is likely to do the same.

At one company, the CEO asked a president of a business unit to lead the company-wide culture change initiative. The business unit president was excited by the challenge, and she took it on with enthusiasm. She assembled a team of representatives from each of the lines of business and, with them, researched assessment instruments to measure the current corporate culture and the desired future culture. With that information in hand, the team mapped out the process for changing the organization's culture.

At another company, the Human Resources Vice President worked with the CEO to enable culture change. In this case, the people processes needed a complete overhaul, so this HR executive was perfectly positioned to enact change from her area of expertise. Later, we'll discuss the importance of people processes in building and maintaining a vibrant culture. Always remember that culture reflects how you treat your employees, which suggests that examining people processes is a good place to start making improvements that will shape your culture.

The transformation process is as follows:

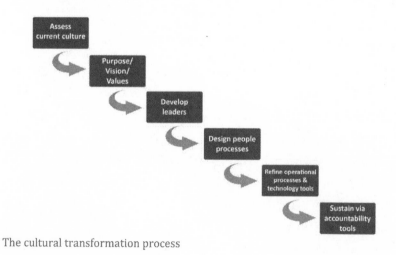

The cultural transformation process

Assess Current and Desired Culture

To make a sustainable change, a project manager needs to study the current situation and create a benchmark against which to measure future improvements. It is no different with a company cultural transformation effort. You can consider multiple options for assessing and benchmarking your current and desired cultures.

In organizational studies, a researcher typically chooses a quantitative, qualitative, or hybrid approach to assessing the current situation. Quantitative approaches attempt to measure aspects of the culture.

Quantitative assessments are typically delivered through online surveys for both leaders, employees and may even include the organization's customers. Survey participants are asked to rate various aspects of the culture, using a variety of techniques. Qualitative approaches, in contrast, are based on interviews, conversations, stories, and observations. A hybrid approach combines both qualitative and quantitative techniques.

There are many quantitative culture assessments on the market today, and each has its strengths. In our consulting practice, we choose the best assessment for the situation from several in our portfolio. Researchers conclude that there is no one best cultural assessment; rather, it depends on what you want to measure or what cultural typology you best resonate with. (Jung et al. 2009, 1090)

Some company culture experts warn against using any surveys and typologies in assessing culture. Schein warns against any prescriptive cultural assessment, saying that typologies "can be quite useless if we are trying to understand one particular organization" (2010, 158). Instead, he recommends a qualitative approach, based on interviews, observations, and examination of cultural artifacts, such as policies and procedures, along with people processes documentation and other tangible evidence of culture.

Quantitative culture assessments produce data, which is critical to twenty-first-century managers' decision-making.

Schein notwithstanding, quantitative culture assessments have their place in your quiver of cultural "arrows" or tools. They produce data, which is critical to twenty-first-century managers' decision-making. Without data, many executives will dismiss results as suspect.

A hybrid approach may be the best option and is the tack we recommend in the assessment phase. You can design a hybrid assessment by combining the results of a data-based survey with interviews, focus groups, and observations of the company.

An online search of cultural assessments will produce a wide array of options. Here are some criteria to use in choosing the quantitative assessment that's right for you:

- Does it have both a current and desired culture measurement? Participants' desired or ideal culture is too important to omit. It's great to measure your current situation against a standard, but if you don't have an idea of where you want to go, how can you get there?

- Be suspicious of any assessment that compares you to one perfect culture. As we've established already, there is no such thing as one perfect culture, nor are there four or five, or any finite number. Each culture is unique, and the measurement you choose should reflect that.

- Is the assessment based on a typology or framework that you can understand and, more importantly, explain to others?

- Does it measure what is important to you?

- Is the instrument based on research, and have its results been statistically validated? Are you convinced of the veracity of the reports produced?

Purpose and Values

In the second phase of a cultural transformation, we suggest that you reexamine or create three strategic statements:

1. A purpose or mission statement

2. A vision statement

3. A values and corresponding behaviors statement

A thorough description of these statements and how to define them are found in a later chapter.

Leadership Development

Once your purpose and value statements have been established, how can you get the leadership team to model the way? The fastest way to derail your culture change project is to tolerate managerial behaviors that detract from the values you develop. Therefore, the most important aspect of cultural transformation is to ensure that managers' actions support the values that the organization espouses. In other words, leaders must walk the talk, not just pay lip service to the ideals. In many cases, this requires either a change in how the existing leaders lead or a change of leaders.

We recommend a combination of experientially based classroom training, individual coaching, and group follow-up discussions to structure your leadership development program. Large corporations will develop their own programs, tailored to their unique needs and industry, with the help of their in-house training and development team. Midsized and smaller companies, or departments within a company, may need to engage the services of a third-party training-and-coaching firm to assist in creating this essential program. In any case, the leadership development process could follow these steps:

1. Start with a 360-degree or a combination of 360-degree and individual assessments to raise the coaching client's **Leaders must walk the talk, not just pay lip service to the company ideals.** (in this case, the manager's) self-awareness and create a baseline against which to measure improvements.

2. Match each client with either an internal or external executive coach. The coach should be trained and credentialed through the International Coach Federation or another reputable institution.

3. With knowledge gained from the assessment step, the client and coach create a development

The

x

plan with goals for leadership growth and action steps to achieve them.

4. Each coaching client attends a curriculum of training based on his/her specific needs, as identified in the assessment step. Both beginning and advanced topics may be needed. The media for training delivery (in-person, via interactive webinar or online) is not as important as the follow-up coaching that holds participants accountable to their action items.

5. Training modules might include the following topics, divided into basic and advanced topics (Hildebrandt and Webb 2016):

Basic managerial training topics	Advanced training topics
• New manager foundations	• Influence across the organization
• Communication skills	• Leadership presence
• Building effective teams	• Emotional intelligence
• Delegation skills	• Managing up the organization
• Time management skills	• Prioritizing workload

Basic managerial training topics	Advanced training topics
• Coaching and developing team members	• Mindfulness and stress management
• Conflict management	
• Designing effective work processes	
• Leading teams through change	

6. The coach and client should meet regularly (at least every other week) during the coaching process to discuss strategies, measure progress, and hold the client accountable to action steps.

7. The end of coaching is marked by conducting a survey of the original 360-degree participants to measure the client's behavioral changes and skills acquisition. Results are shared with both the client and boss, ensuring that the boss can continue further development efforts with the client.

Design Operational Processes and Technology Tools

To build and sustain a vibrant culture, leaders must consider the efficacy of their operational processes. What good is it to spend time and effort establishing values, purpose, vision, and leadership development if your operational procedures are inefficient or overly complicated? Leaders possess a powerful motivational tool: the ability to enable work progress, every day. Employees don't want to come to work to fail—to the contrary, they need to feel that they make progress toward a goal on a regular basis. Fine-tuned operational processes facilitate the satisfaction of accomplishing tasks that advance the organization's goals, whereas inefficient processes demotivate employees, taking away from the positive values of the company, and reducing productivity. In subsequent chapters, we'll discover how to assess your current processes and streamline them to motivate your workforce.

Hand-in-glove with operational processes are the technology tools that you provide workers to accomplish their tasks. As you redefine your operational processes, updates and changes to the

Leaders possess a powerful motivational tool: the ability to enable work progress, every day.

technology tools employed in producing work must be considered. Long ago, I learned from my father what every do-it-yourself handyman knows: using the correct tool for the job makes the task easier and the results better. Your computer systems are the tools of the twenty-first-century worker. Ensure they are the best you can afford.

Sustain the Culture via Accountability Systems

Accountability systems include several managerial actions, such as the following:

- Creating a cadence for setting annual goals and cascading them down to departments and individuals
- Tracking and rewarding goal achievements
- Establishing key performance indicators
- Creating company-wide and department-specific dashboard reports
- Developing individual performance systems to guide and reward employee development

Remember, everything you do either contributes to or detracts from the company culture. In this book, we'll ask you to look at everything you do as a company through the lens of culture.

A Culture Change Initiative:
Salmon Sims Thomas

Salmon Sims Thomas, an accounting firm in Dallas, TX, offers an instructive example of how to work through the cultural transformation process. The founder of the firm had recently retired, and the new CEO, Bill Sims, wished to make his mark, leaving his legacy with the firm. He was particularly concerned with the culture of the company, which he felt was not as positive as it could be even though the firm had implemented a highly successful culture in the past. Sims suspected that some aspects of the organization's culture were the cause of both high turnover of good employees and stalled revenue growth. When he invited me to discuss how we could improve the culture, I explained the cultural transformation process, starting with an assessment of the current culture and creation of an action plan that would drive the company to a better future state.

We jumped into the first phase of the process with gusto. We invited all employees to participate in an online assessment of the current and desired culture, interviewed key executives in the company, and conducted focus groups of representatives from all departments within the company. Bringing the leadership team together, we presented the results of the assessment and proposed a thirty-six-step action plan that included the creation of values for the company, executive coaching for the C-suite, and a program of leadership development for rising managers.

Sims convened a values steering committee, composed of enthusiastic and influential employees from each department. This group defined and introduced the values, behaviors, and metrics that would serve to guide the firm into the future. The CEO, who was active in the values steering committee, assumed responsibility for key value communications to the workforce, including recognizing those team members who exemplified the values at each month's staff lunch. Eileen Keller, another partner, took responsibility for refining departmental processes to ensure that both tools and work instructions were up-to-date and optimal.

Things got worse before they got better for this company—a common phenomenon when the culture changes.

Things got worse before they got better for this company—a common phenomenon when the culture changes. The firm lost several key employees in the transition, including two partners.

Sims wisely remarked to me that the employees he lost were not the ones that could uphold the values and contribute positively to the new culture. Even so, given the region's extremely low unemployment rate, it was painful to see the key contributors leave the firm and difficult to replace them. It got so bad that on the day of the annual leadership off-site meeting, Sims came home from work and his wife asked, "Did anyone else quit today?" Ironically, that was the day that one of the partners left the firm, announcing in an email to Bill that not only was he not attending the leadership team meeting, but also, he wasn't coming back to work.

With the help of one-on-one coaching, the members of the executive suite strengthened their leadership resolve, communicating openly and transparently to the staff throughout the transition. During this time, Sims remarked,

"People will resist a change, but the leader's job is to cast the vision and get out of the way."

He noted that communication and trust were vital to the change initiative, saying "you communicate your vision and hope that people trust you enough to follow. I ask them to act into the feeling, meaning, Follow the values-based behaviors we've established, and you'll eventually get the feeling of what we are striving for."

Sims focused on people and systems to change the culture. "You have to get the right people and help them do what they do best," he says. He set up committees of interested staff members to oversee the changes, such as how to implement a new accounting system for the firm, which enabled an organizational change that combined the internal accounting and customer bookkeeping teams.

One complaint heard during the culture assessment was that there wasn't a clear path to promotion in this firm nor was there a program to develop high-potential employees' leadership skills. The partners created the *Salmon Sims Thomas Executive Leadership Institute*, a training and group coaching program to facilitate and accelerate the education of high-potential employees and future partners of the firm. The executive team committed the firm to refining its recruiting/development/coaching programs as an investment in the sustainability of the company, training the leaders of tomorrow.

Slowly, over the course of two painful years, the ship righted itself and the firm is now poised to experience smoother waters within the next fiscal year. Interestingly, throughout all these difficult changes, the company experienced a small percentage increase in both revenues and profitability.

Sims says, "Our goal is to achieve fifteen percent annual revenue growth for the next ten years—and now I think we have a solid chance of making it!"

Key Concepts

1. Transforming a company culture takes time that is measured in years.

2. Like any change initiative, it is best to start with a current situation analysis and benchmark. The cultural transformation process starts with analysis of the current and desired cultures, proceeding to core values creation or refinement.

3. Expect a bumpy ride for the first phase of your culture change initiative. It is normal to lose employees, either through voluntary or involuntary turnover, who can't or don't wish to make the change with you.

4. Leadership development is the most powerful driver of cultural change. When your leaders consistently lead in a manner that supports the core values while demanding accountability to expectations, the culture will change.

5. Like Bill Sims, focus on systems and people. Follow the *Company Culture Ecosystem* to embed values into all aspects of your company.

Case Study Interlude: Share on Purpose

Establishing Core Values from the Start

Share on Purpose is a holding company or incubator for a portfolio of small, rapid-growth companies in the business service industry. In the portfolio are a media company, a training company and a small company growth consultancy. Led by a highly successful serial entrepreneur, Terri Maxwell, this company is intent on building a positive culture from the inception of any of its portfolio companies. As the leader of the consultancy group, Laura Armbruster, said,

"We have to build the culture NOW when we are small, because it's much harder to undo a culture that you've built unconsciously."

All workers at Share on Purpose are virtual, meaning they work at home and travel to the company's small office only for a weekly team meeting. All other meetings are held via phone or webinar, including the Monday morning leadership meetings and team meetings. Maxwell insists on Monday morning meetings to get everyone focused on the week's work:

"That's an important thing, to demark the weekend from the week, especially in a virtual environment. You can lose

productivity if you ease into the workweek. The Monday morning meetings are focused and upbeat."

In addition to Monday morning meetings, each employee has brief weekly meetings with both their manager and their clients. Regarding the rhythm of weekly meetings, CEO Terri Maxwell remarked,

"People are more efficient here. They think it's due to working virtually, but it's really because of the structure we've created."

At Share on Purpose, the weekly/monthly/quarterly annual meeting schedule creates a structure that Maxwell has found to enhance productivity.

The company created a "core team," comprised of representatives from each of the portfolio companies. This team is

Acrylic painting of company core values

responsible for upholding culture and creating a mindset for the company. For example, the core team was instrumental in establishing a four-and-a-half-day work week in which no meetings are scheduled on Friday afternoons.

Two artifacts of their culture were a wall display of acrylic paintings employees created of the company core values, and the guiding principles of the company posted on the refrigerator in the kitchen. Each of the values was depicted in graphic form on separate canvases and was painted by small groups of employees at a company party held at a wine and painting shop.

The company's values form the acronym SHARE: Supportive, Hopeful, Authentic, Resourceful, and Enthusiastic. Of the companies I researched, only at this company were employees able to recite the company's core values. Each of the employees interviewed started with the acronym SHARE and could remember what each letter stood for.

I observed a Thursday team meeting in the office and attended a "Purpose Party" that the company held at a local restaurant in the late afternoon for team members of all the portfolio companies. The company paid for appetizers and drinks for everyone. They hold a Purpose Party monthly, and attendance is voluntary. The goals of the meeting included are to provide a face-to-face event so people can socialize across the portfolio companies, update employees on internal news like promotions, and award winners of the peer recognition program a Starbucks gift card worth $10.

HAPPY MONDAYS

CHAPTER 4

Values and Purpose

Is it possible to have a positive company culture without defining core values? Of course, yes. If the founders of a company are congruent in their behaviors and what they stand for in the world, it is their example that will set and carry the culture. The exciting start-up company that I described in the preface of this book is a great example of a vibrant culture that needed no stated core values; rather, the strong guidance of the founders and their small leadership team was enough to exemplify the values and behaviors for the team. After having grown bigger, however, the leaders recognized the need to codify what the company stood for and created core values. Although a magic number is difficult to propose, once a company gets past about forty employees, it is almost impossible to communicate and exemplify the implicit values and acceptable behaviors without stating them.

And, as Richard Barrett wisely observes, "When values are not defined, the culture of the organization is subject to the vagaries of the personality of the leader. When the leader changes, the values will change" (104).

This represents a risk for any company. In the absence of espoused values, it is likely that a change in leadership will bring with it new values for better or worse. More than that, explicitly stated values are needed to communicate, embed, and hold people accountable to the standards you wish to uphold in your organization. Therefore, I recommend to

Make your values memorable, a few (five to seven), pertinent to the business, and emotionally evocative.

all my clients that they define core values and their supporting behaviors.

We are all aware of the rock-star companies that live by their values, including Zappos, Southwest Airlines, Steelcase, Whole Foods, and Container Store. In the companies that I have studied, it was a mixed bag when it came to explicitly stated values.

There are some caveats about values: make them memorable, few (five to seven), pertinent to the business, and emotionally evocative. Typically, companies state values as a list of nouns, but I've seen verbs used successfully in value statements. Distill your values to no more than seven to increase the odds they will be remembered by all employees.

One way to aid memory of values is to create an acronym of these values.

For example, Schneider Electric, a multi-national electrical products corporation, uses the acronym SCOPE to describe their values.

SCOPE stands for Straightforward, Challenge, Open, Passionate, and Effective. CompuCom has the WIRE values (Win/win, Integrity, Respect, and Excellence). McKesson created the I CARE values: Integrity, Customer-first, Accountability, Respect, Excellence.

In these companies, the acronym aids employees' recall of the values. In my research, only at Share on Purpose could employees remember the company's core values. The formulation of the values into a meaningful acronym, SHARE, was the key to memory. During interviews, the employees would literally start with the acronym and retrofit the value words into it.

Instead of espoused values, Alkali Insurance articulated ten best habits, which none of the interviewees could remember. In examining their ten best habits, I found the habits could be distilled to five or six underlying values. Remember how important it is to create just a few memorable values.

Another company had just a purpose statement and no stated core values. In the two companies that did not have stated values, there were positive values in evidence, indicating that core values are not mandatory to produce productive behaviors.

Most importantly, all the large companies I interviewed had explicitly stated core values, lending credence to the recommendation to define core values as soon as possible in the growth of a company.

How to Create Core Values

A complete process document on how to conduct a core values workshop can be found on Brio Leadership's website (www.brioleadership.com/resources.html). The basic concepts are included here.

The best core values follow these guidelines. They are as follows:

- Memorable (consider formulating an acronym of the values)
- No more than five to seven values
- Pertinent to the business
- Emotionally evocative

Gather your leadership team and ask them what values they wish to honor in this company. Once you have a list of five or six, check them to see if your top performers exemplify these values. What are you missing or should eliminate?

The most important step is to define both the behaviors that detract from and the behaviors that support each value, plus the metrics that measure the supporting behaviors.

This list of behaviors and metrics will become inputs into your organization's People Practices such as new hire interview forms, performance reviews, and recognition templates.

You might use a form like the following:

Core value	Definition/ Description	Behaviors that detract	Behaviors that support	Metrics for supportive behaviors
1.				
2.				
3.				
4.				
5.				

Benefits of Purpose Statements

Purpose statements have become a de facto standard in companies today and typically are a substitute for mission statements. The purpose of these statements is to define the *raison d'etre* or the reason for the existence of your company. It defines the higher goals of the organization and what it will do to make a difference in the world.

The purpose statement identifies the intersection of the answers to these two questions for your organization:

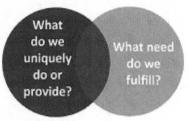

1. What do we uniquely do or provide?

2. What need do we fulfill?

Your company's purpose lies in the overlap between these two concerns.

It is well-known that the millennial generation yearns to work at a company that has a purpose higher than making money. However, people of all generations not only yearn but also *deserve* to do work that is both meaningful and impactful. Knowing how everyone's contribution moves the company forward toward its purpose is key to employee engagement and satisfaction. Because of this, it is important to define your purpose.

The purpose defines the *raison d'etre*, the reason for the existence of the company.

Some examples of purpose statements are as follows:

- **Brio Leadership:** To ensure people are happy to go to work on Monday mornings.

- **BMW:** To enable people to experience the joy of driving.

- **Interstate Batteries:** To glorify God and enrich lives as we deliver the most trustworthy source of power to the world.

- **Merck:** To preserve and improve human life.

- **Disney:** To use our imaginations to bring happiness to millions.

To use a personal example of how remembering your purpose is motivational, I'll tell a story about the writing of this book. Any author knows how difficult and time-consuming it is to write a book, and I exhibited all the writer's blocks, procrastination techniques, and false starts that you can imagine.

I had worked with several coaches about my inability to sit down and just crank out this book, to no avail. I was stuck. All I could think about were the business benefits of authoring a book. About three weeks into a six-week writing workshop in which I was supposed to finish my book, I remembered that my purpose in creating this book was: to share the wisdom that I have learned in my years as a manager and consultant and to increase the number of people excited to go to work on Monday mornings. Once I placed my purpose forefront in my mind, I felt a palpable shift in my energy, and I finished the book in a matter of days.

How can you use a purpose higher than making money to inspire and motivate your team?

Sidebar Conversation: Culture Champions

Role of the Culture Champion at Case Study Companies

At the companies I researched, there was a designated person in charge of cultural activities, a role commonly called a "culture champion." In three of the companies, this person also held an administrative role. At Alkali, this person bore the title of "Strategic Assistant." She conducted the initial, culture-based interview of all hiring candidates and suggested what topic the CEO should address during the "Steve Speaks" portion of the monthly Team Growth meetings. At Marketwave as well as at Acuity Systems, the culture champion was the administrative assistant. In contrast, the culture champion role at Share on Purpose was shared among a portfolio company's president, the CFO and the administrative assistant.

Because meetings and social events require detailed planning, it stands to reason that putting responsibility for handling logistical details in the hands of an administrator increases the probability of the events proceeding smoothly and regularly. Indeed, at one company, an employee remarked that their monthly dinners had been erratic, but she hoped that the newly hired administrative assistant would schedule them regularly.

At both large companies, there was a manager in charge of the culture. One had a position called "Queen of Laughter and Fun," while the other large company used the title of "Culture Ambassador." At BerylHealth, the chief culture person chaired the culture committee, which planned cultural activities such as large group meetings, "reward and recognition, on boarding, communication, our BerylCares program, community service, and events" (Spiegelman 2012). The BerylCares program was an employee hardship fund, funded through employees'' voluntary contributions of one or two dollars per paycheck. The culture committee at that company created the guidelines for awarding hardship funds to employee applicants and evaluated each application accordingly. The practice of creating a culture committee was echoed at Share on Purpose Company, where the core team oversaw protecting the culture. Share on Purpose had representatives from each of the portfolio companies, and its purpose was a dual one, per CEO Terri Maxwell:

"Half of the purpose {of the core team} is to make the culture better, and the other is to make themselves personally a better person."

As an example of how Share on Purpose's core team members explore ways to improve themselves, the CEO mentioned that she recently worked with the team to increase their "abundance mentality" through training and personal exercises.

Key Concepts

1. Define your core values according to the values that the current leadership team wishes to honor. Then check the list against the characteristics of your best employees.

2. Once defined, it is easy to relegate core values to a digital file on your network drive and forget them. Instead, define the behaviors that both support and detract from the core values by department. For example, the behaviors of a sales team might differ from the accounting team. Then, use those behaviors as input into new hire interviews, performance reviews and termination decisions.

3. Because sustaining a culture takes discipline, it is important to delegate the tactical tasks of scheduling meetings, planning, and preparing the rituals, etc. In smaller companies, this can be a person; in larger organizations, it usually is a Culture Committee or Culture Champions. This person or committee can help ensure the regularity of both meetings and rituals within them. Remember that team members notice and interpret a missed meeting or the absence of a ritual as an indication that it wasn't important enough to schedule and execute.

4. Structure the culture committee to work closely with the CEO for direction and

coaching. Remember culture is set at the top, so the time the CEO spends with the culture committee is time well spent.

5. Consider creating an acronym of your values. One company's values formed the acronym SHARE, and it was the only company in our research at which all employees could recite the core values.

Case Study Interlude: BKM Total Office of Texas

Positive Leadership

Twenty years ago, Carol Roehrig was an executive in the Steelcase office in Minneapolis, MN. Her employer, the premier supplier of office furniture and innovative design, had a pattern of purchasing companies that distribute its products and placing their most promising managers as CEO of the acquired companies. Steelcase had bought BKM Total Office, which had multiple offices across the US, and invited Carol to be the CEO of the Dallas-based business. From these auspicious beginnings, Carol has refined her leadership and grown the company ten-fold.

BKM Total Office of Texas creates innovative workplaces to enrich human connections in offices, hospitals and schools. A leading Steelcase distributor, BKM's services include design, project management, installation, warehousing and furniture refurbishment.

Due to their commitment to designing and implementing work spaces that facilitate employee engagement, management has stated that culture is important to them. This company holds quarterly all-hands

BKM's training & meeting room

meetings. The purpose of this meeting is to educate employees on the financial performance of the company, apprise them of the status of ongoing projects and new initiatives, highlight customer loyalty ratings and compliments from customers, and celebrate recent installations by showing pictures of the finished project, which many in the company may never have had a chance to see in person.

In correcting, the leader walks a fine line between scolding, which can be de-motivating, and inspiring employees to do better. Roehrig walked that line skillfully when she discussed the importance of tracking error rates (called open issues) and customer satisfaction comments. She motivated people by turning what could be viewed as a negative into a positive:

"It's really important about the feedback we receive. The coaches that made the biggest difference in our lives are the ones who corrected us. If you're associated with a complaint, thank the customer because it will help us get better. Some of you get irked about open issues. If we don't figure out the why or root cause of an open issue, {it could affect a customer}. We do this {track open issues} so we can be corrected before they correct us. Open issues are a score of us, not of an individual. We need to learn from feedback."

The skill with which she delivered this message was confirmed by feedback received from the culture champion on how the CEO's comments affected her:

"{The CEO} was brilliant in how she phrased the introduction of open issues, it turned out really positive. That was so motivating".

BKM Total Office of Texas' corporate offices double as the company's showroom, meant to demonstrate that the latest trends in office configurations and furniture work well for a functioning organization.  This is clearly a case of eating your own dog food! The office layout is open; managers have high-walled cubicles.

BKM's open office

The company has strict rules about how each employee's desk must look.

For example, a minimum of personal items can be displayed, no hand-written signs are allowed, etc. The training room, where the meeting I observed was held, is large enough to hold all attendees when the chairs are set up in auditorium style and has modern accoutrements such as modular white boards, a ceiling-hung projector, and colorful desks and chairs. Every care is taken to maintain the office space as a trendy but professional environment.

An annual ritual at BKM is to create and share a Holiday Video. Produced in-house by its creative marketing team, the video is sent to all clients and posted on the internet. One employee reported:

"The holiday video is fun and enjoyable. Everyone has a good time. People are dancing around the showroom floor. I can remember all of the last five videos!"

Although the video is ostensibly created as a Christmas greeting card to clients and vendors, it is also a clever way of showing the capabilities of BKM as an innovative office design company. BKM's office is also BKM's showroom.

CHAPTER 5

Leadership

The leader of a company has a deeply influential role in embedding cultural values and setting the emotional tone for the company. Therefore, leadership is the first tactical element of the *Company Culture Ecosystem*, and the element of culture that has the most leverage. If you can improve leadership abilities throughout the company, you will automatically improve the culture. Leaders carry that much weight.

When we facilitate leadership development training, we start with a module on leadership basics. Can you remember when you were a new, first-time manager (perhaps you are in that situation currently)? Remember how scary that was? Suddenly, you don't work with your buddies and chums; rather, you work with employees who report to you—and may resent you. You no longer are judged on how you get your work done, but on how well you get work done through others. You must transition from managing just your own workload, to assigning and overseeing the workload of a team.

Leadership Starts from Here

All leaders should consider taking a "servant leader" stance with the team. This concept, conceived by John Greenleaf (2001), states that leaders serve their teams, not the opposite. A mature leader will consider the well-being of her team before her own and will wonder about how she can enable the team to improve, advance their careers, and feel fulfillment in their work. The servant leader will ask the team members, "How can I help you?" Another technique of servant leaders is to "run interference" for, or protect, their teams from unnecessary politicking in the organization. They take the heat from upper management or the board, taking responsibility for their team's shortcomings while sharing the credit when things go well. They are selective in sharing criticisms with the team and refrain from relaying petty gossip they hear about anyone or anything in the organization. In this way, the servant leader acts like a wise parent.

Here's a secret that all managers should utilize: assume positive intent. This short phrase, which you should burn into your brain, reminds you to assume that people are trying to do a good job, even when they don't do a good job, or when you are mystified as to what on earth they were trying to do. This attitude is a lot like the Theory X and Theory Y management theory of the 1980s (McGregor 2006). Theory X assumes that workers are lazy, selfish, and don't care about their jobs, therefore needing to be managed closely and only monetarily incentivized to be productive. Theory Y, on the other hand, assumes that employees want to do a good job, are intrinsically creative and resourceful, and, given the end goal, can figure out how to do a job with minimal oversight.

If you assume positive intent, you can avoid locking into an "us" vs. "them" mentality that always gums up the works in an organization. For example, if your counterpart in another department approaches you to do some work for them and you assume positive intent, you will ask probing questions trying to understand the underlying need

As the leader of your team, you become a role model for your people, who will instinctively follow the example you set.

and will seek to find a win-win situation for both departments. If you assume negative intent, you lock yourself into stories that may or may not be true, as in "Those lazy, good-for-nothing people, they are trying to push their work off on us again!" With that approach, you put up roadblocks, act obstreperously, and poison the relationship with the other

61

department. This can only result in lost productivity due to low interdepartmental teamwork.

As the leader of your team, you become a role model for your organization. You are now the alpha dog of the pack, and people will instinctually follow the example you set. Do you want your team to show up on time? Then you must show up on time. Do you want your team to treat each other with respect? Then you must always treat others respectfully. In fact, you have little room for slacking off, because your team will examine, discuss, and dissect your every move, facial expression, and voice inflection you make.

To illustrate how a team notices everything its leader does: in one department of a large company, the manager was emotionally volatile and could make life miserable for the team. Her employees knew that if she was in a bad mood, you'd best avoid her or else you could be the victim of her harsh tongue. Conversely, if she was in a good mood, everyone had a great day and work got done pleasantly.

The team created a mechanism whereby they could assess the boss's mood soon after she arrived in the morning. They called it the "canary call," named for the bird that coal miners would lower into a mineshaft to determine if the air was fit to breathe. If the canary came back alive, it was safe to work that day. If not, no go. The team chose one person, which rotated each morning, to visit the boss in her office, chat with her, and determine what mood she was in. Then, the spy would secretly send an email to everyone in the department—except the boss—with a mood report. If the mood was poor, people knew it would be a bad day and to avoid the boss. If the mood was good, everyone breathed a sigh of relief and prepared for a pleasant day. This story reflects how strongly the boss's mood and attitude influences the well-being of the entire team.

To guard against unwittingly influencing the mood of your team, you can heighten your self-awareness by considering the following questions: What facial expression am I wearing? What was my tone of voice, my body language? Could people tell that I was nervous/scared/angry? Did I control the expression of my emotions to best outcome? Did I communicate news sufficiently?

The most important step an effective manager can make is to transition from a "me" mentality to a "we" mentality. At first, the concept of "we" will focus on your team and how to help them achieve results. A good supervisor will ask herself, "How can I help my team do its work?"

As a manager matures and gains more responsibility, she will need to take on a broader purview, that of the entire company. A good manager will ask herself, "What can I do to benefit the whole company?" And, as she becomes an executive, her concept of "we" needs to include all the stakeholders of the business: employees, suppliers, customers, stockholders, and the community.

The executive's question now must be: "How can I balance the competing interests of all of our stakeholders and make the best decision for the system?"

Leadership and Relationship

It is said that employees join companies but leave managers. That means that the reputation of the company attracts good people, but to retain star performers, leaders must be effective and constructive. The B2B Approved Index found that almost half of employee turnover was due to an unsatisfactory relationship with the boss (Higginbottom 2015). Still another survey found that the characteristic they most value in a manager is a caring attitude.

All these reports indicate that to lead well is to be in relationship with people. Essentially, leaders must show they care. They need to take the time to know and understand their team members. They must communicate openly and honestly with them. Let's look at some important findings from Dr. John

Gottman (2001, 15) who has studied relationships for decades.

In reviewing videotapes of married couples conversing, Gottman has established a "magic ratio" of five positive comments to every negative remark as the way to build a strong relationship. Within five minutes of watching the video, the doctor can predict which marriages will fail and which ones will be successful.

> Leaders can use the "magic ratio" of five positive comments to every negative one to build a strong relationship with team members.

What he watches for is the "magic ratio": do both people in the marriage relationship offer five positive comments about the other person to every negative said? If yes, the marriage will likely endure (Lisita 2012).His findings can be applied to relationships in the workplace as well.

Before you earn the right to criticize someone, either in the workplace or in your personal life, the "magic ratio" recommends you express five positive comments or actions toward that person. In this way, you build a constructive relationship and ensure that the organizational culture is positive.

Gottman also identifies four negative behaviors that will doom a relationship, calling them the Four Horsemen of the Apocalypse.

In Gottman's application, the Four Horsemen predict the end of a professional or personal relationship. The four destructive behaviors are criticism, contempt, defensiveness, and stonewalling. When these are present in a workplace, the result is a negative, unproductive culture. Let's examine these four actions and how they show up in the workplace.

Criticism

There is a fine line between constructive and destructive feedback. Constructive feedback always assumes positive intent, whereas destructive criticism assumes either maliciousness or stupidity of the other person. Destructive criticism often includes the words "you," "never," and "always," as in "You are always undermining my credibility in the quarterly meeting."

> **Destructive criticism often includes the words "you," "never," and "always."**

That criticism could be expressed constructively in this way: "I understand that we are all trying to put our best foot forward in the meeting with the CEO, but I felt humiliated when you persisted in questioning my recommendations."

Note that the rephrase starts with an assumption of positive and communal intent ("We are all trying to put our best foot forward") and ends with an "I" statement that names the felt emotion ("I felt humiliated..."). A powerful humility (note the paradox in that phrase) is created when you do this. By starting with a positive assumption and ending by voicing your true feelings, you humanize both yourself and the other person, thus creating a prelude to a productive conversation.

Betty (not her real name) had a highly critical boss who nearly caused her to quit her job. More than once, he dropped an assignment on her desk at 4:00 p.m. on a Friday.

He attached a sticky note to a pile of papers with the words, "I need this report on my desk by the time I get in on Monday morning."

Betty labored all weekend on the report and emailed it to the boss late on Sunday night. By the time she arrived on Monday morning, tired from the weekend's work, she found the report on her chair, printed from the email she sent the night before. The report was littered with red marks and comments from the boss, much like a teacher's critique of a student's term paper, criticizing the report and demanding that it be corrected that day.

Unsurprisingly, Betty suffered high stress in this relationship and developed a serious medical condition that forced her to take extensive sick leave for treatment. Fortunately for her, the boss ultimately left the company, and she could continue her employment with a less toxic manager.

Contempt

Contempt is the opposite of respect. Contemptuous words or actions are mean-spirited, with the objective of making the other person feel worthless, stupid, and despised. The techniques of contempt are ridicule, mocking, sarcasm. They can be expressed with either words or body language, such as eye rolling.

It sounds like this: "I can't believe you screwed up this order again. Haven't I told you a million times how to handle this? Are you stupid or something?"

Contempt is devastating to a professional relationship because the attacker assumes a superiority to the accused person.

As a manager, you may not blatantly express contempt for a person because that behavior is rarely tolerated in a professional environment, but you may assume a mental attitude of contempt toward someone. Monitor your thoughts and feelings toward others to guard against letting that attitude slip out in your dealings with this person. Once it is released, it can't be retrieved, and it will damage the relationship.

Defensiveness

Defensiveness shows up in the workplace in the form of shirking responsibility for your own mistakes, laying blame on another person, or making excuses for poor performance. These ensure that the manager who uses them will be feared but not respected. It sounds like:

"If I had a team of high performers working for me, this type of mistake wouldn't happen."

Woe to the leader who feels and expresses defensiveness toward her team. She will reap rewards in the form of lack of trust, low productivity, and possibly high turnover.

Stonewalling

In Gottman's terminology, stonewalling is shutting down all communications, ignoring the other person and avoiding dealing with the presenting issue. Although sometimes it is best to take time to collect your thoughts before dealing with a performance or relationship issue on your team, the leader who refuses to deal with it only makes the situation worse. Again, the results of this behavior are detrimental to the effectiveness of the team.

Characteristics of Effective Leaders

The following are the seven principal characteristics that an effective leader should cultivate. We'll discuss each one in turn.

7 characteristics of effective leaders

Self-awareness

A leader must first understand himself so he can understand others. Only by continually seeking more information about the self can you become an effective leader. If you can't recognize an emotion, personality quirk, or tendency in yourself, how can you size up other people? The more you focus on increasing your self-awareness and self-knowledge, the better person you become. And the more well-rounded and mature person you become, the better leader you are. A good place to start is with personality and strengths assessments. There are several free or low-cost assessments that you can take yourself and receive rudimentary results, including Myers-Briggs Type Indicator and StrengthsFinder. An experienced executive coach or Human Resources representative can help you obtain a deeper understanding of your results.

One of my coaching clients has done an exemplary job of noticing his emotions and modulating his reactions to them. He did this by monitoring himself throughout a workday, constantly asking himself mentally, "How did I handle that situation?" If he wasn't pleased with his actions, words, or results, he would gently consider what he might do better in the future. If he did well, he congratulated himself.

Another technique that works is taking time at the beginning or end of the day to review the previous day and plan for the coming one. Leaders who practice this use the same technique as my client in the previous example, but in retrospect. As they review their calendar and what happened that day, they ask themselves "How did I handle that situation?" and either congratulate themselves or think of a better way to handle it in the future.

Journaling, or simply jotting down a note or two, about the day is another effective technique to increase self-awareness. One of my executive coaching clients has kept a journal for over ten years. In his journal is a page for every day of the year and on that page, there are ten sets of four blank lines, one set for every year. Every night, he writes a handful of sentences about where he was that day, what he was doing and some highlights. One year, he told his wife that he would be out of town for her birthday. She complained that he was ALWAYS traveling on her birthday. He went back to his journal, turned to the page of her birthday, and happily reported to her that he had been out of town for only two of the past seven birthdays, but he was still sorry that he'd have to miss her special day this year.

Lastly, aggressively seeking feedback helps a leader understand how he is viewed by others. There are several ways to do this. One is to make a pact with a peer or colleague to observe and give constructive criticism to each other after meetings. Another way is to ask team members how you are doing as their manager. This is effective on a semiannual or annual basis, perhaps around performance review times. Suggested questions to start a conversation with your employees are as follows:

- What do I do well, that I should continue to do?
- What don't you like, that I should stop doing?
- What would you like me to start doing?

One of my favorite managers would often say, "Feedback is the breakfast of champions!"

Remember to seek feedback often, and you will always be on the journey of self-improvement as a manager.

Gratitude

As we established above, the art of managing people is getting things done through others, not doing everything yourself. One of the most overlooked techniques you possess to get people to do things is to first notice what they do well and thank them for the good job. Expressing gratitude is a mark of a good manager.

When I was a manager, I liked to send team members handwritten notes to their home addresses, acknowledging a notable achievement on their part and thanking them. Not only does it make the employee's day, but it telegraphs to the whole family that mom/dad/spouse is doing important work at the office.

Empathy

Simon Sinek, in his latest book entitled *Leaders Eat Last,* identifies the criticality of a leader's empathy. Using a military context, he says, "...exceptional organizations all have cultures in which the leaders provide cover from above and the people on the ground look out for each other...the way any organization can achieve this is with *empathy*" (8). (italics are mine).

Empathy, of course, is the ability to imagine what another person is feeling. This ability is made possible by a fascinating phenomenon in the human brain called "mirror neurons." When you observe someone else experiencing a hurt or an emotional upset, cells in your brain activate in the same way they would if you were experiencing it yourself.

Neuroscientists discovered this almost by accident while conducting experiments with monkeys, whose brains perform similarly to humans. In one lab, a monkey was attached to a Functional Magnetic Resonating Image (*f*MRI) machine that records which parts of the brain "light up" or become active at a certain time.

The researcher had taken a break and was eating a banana in front of the monkey. The researcher just happened to notice that, as the monkey watched her, the monkey's brain was activated in the same region as when the monkey himself ate a banana. In other words, by simply observing the act, the monkey's brain reacted as if he was eating the banana. This explains why we might involuntarily wince when we observe someone else crashing into a wall or otherwise hurting themselves. Our brain's neurons are firing in the same pattern as if we were getting hurt ourselves.

Empathy, therefore, is a neurological phenomenon. So why do some people have "more" empathy than others? Although there might be medical or hereditary reasons for varying degrees of empathy, the good news is that empathy, just like every other emotional intelligence skill, can be developed. Our brains continue to regenerate and make new neural connections until the day we die, so we are not stuck with only the gray matter we were born with.

The most important technique in developing empathy is the ability to listen deeply and compassionately to others. This can be accomplished by the following practices:

- Minimizing distractions. Turn away from your computer screen and put away your cell phone when you are speaking to a team member.

- Making and maintaining eye contact with the speaker.

- Showing encouragement by saying things like "hmm," "I see," or "go on" or by nodding your head or smiling.

- If you are having trouble focusing on the speaker, mentally repeat the words you are hearing as they are spoken. Alternatively, mentally visualize what the speaker is describing as you hear what is said.

Trust is built up over time, by making commitments to another person and delivering on them.

To develop empathy, it is important to practice regular pauses or moments of reflection in your day. Take a moment every now and then to mentally stop and review what has just happened or prepare for what is going to happen. One client of mine does this as he walks to and from meetings. Productive self-reflection is the hallmark of an empathetic leader. When faced with a challenging employee or coworker, practice asking yourself the following questions and consider the answers before acting. Here are three questions that will help you develop empathy toward others:

- What emotions could the person be feeling?

- How would I feel if I experienced what they did?

- What could possibly make me to act in the same way?

The trick is to develop your emotional antenna so you can detect the feelings and moods of people you work with and manage your relationships to positive outcome. These questions help you get out of your personal interpretation of what's going on and "walk a mile in the other's shoes"—the essence of empathy.

Trust/Trustworthiness

One of my coaching clients was having serious trouble with her boss. In fact, she sought out coaching because the boss had given her a poor performance review. At one point in the coaching process, I asked her, "What is it about this boss that makes him untrustworthy?"

She replied, "He doesn't trust me to do a good job, so he's always texting me about my decisions, second-guessing me. And, he is not reliable in delivering what he promises, so he is unworthy of my trust."

She perfectly described how trust is a two-way street: you must be trusting of your people and deserving of their trust.

Trust and being trustworthy are multi-faceted leadership traits. Richard Barrett (2014) describes trust as having two major components: character traits and competencies. The character traits include intention (described as caring, transparency, and openness) and integrity (described as honesty, fairness, and authenticity). Competency includes capabilities (described as skills, knowledge, and experience) and results (described as reputation, credibility, and results).

Trust is built up over time, by making commitments to another person and delivering on them. It is based on the track record that is established between two people: has each person done what they said they would do?

If you are having trouble trusting your people, you might want to examine how trustworthy you are to them.

Humility

Jim Collins, in his seminal book, *From Good to Great* (2001), cites the two characteristics of a Level Five leader (the highest level in his scheme) as someone who has both humility and will. His prescription appears to be a paradox: Humility is to put aside your ego and act to uphold the organization's welfare; will is to push forward an agenda. It can be difficult for people in power to cultivate humility.

Power tends to corrupt, as in the saying, "Power corrupts, and absolute power corrupts absolutely."

Practicing humility is a way to combat this tendency. Acting humbly is to:

- Share credit with your team when it succeeds

- Treat all people with respect, even those on the bottom of the hierarchy (like the janitor or administrative assistant)

- Admit your mistakes matter-of-factly and openly

- Apologize when you offend

Tom Niesen, the CEO of Acuity Systems, exemplifies the humility required of a leader. Humility is required to combat the "ivory tower syndrome" so common in executives, in which they isolate themselves from both feedback and bad news. Tom regularly asks for feedback from his employees and doesn't punish them when they give him constructive criticism:

"I'll email the whole company, admit that this and that went wrong, and I'll ask for their advice. I'll ask, how do you think I handled this situation? Depending on what the feedback is, I'll either agree or I'll say, I don't know."

Generosity

Managers who are generous with their employees operate from a servant leader's heart, a humble heart. They know that their success is entirely based on the efforts and successes of their team, and they desire to show appreciation through generosity.

In the early days of a small start-up company, the founder hired a promising and talented young woman into an entry-level position. At the time, their company health insurance benefits did not start until thirty days after the employment date. This young woman was involved in a serious car accident during the waiting period and was without health-care coverage. The founder of the company called her in the hospital and promised her that the company would cover all her medical expenses. His generosity completely overwhelmed her, and she dissolved into tears. Not only did the company pay for her health-care bills but also someone from the office called her every day, plus the company organized dinners brought to her home and help with household chores.

Over the next thirty years, the company went public and became the premier provider in its industry, making many people wealthy, including the woman in the car accident. She is now the Senior Vice President of Human Resources for the same, now very large, corporation. When asked about how the company's manner of handling her car accident affected her in the long run, she said:

"It made me two hundred percent loyal to the company and the ideals we stand for. I have given my heart and soul to this company, making sure that we treat all employees like I was treated in the early days." This is the fruit of generosity: Recipients tend to give it back and pay it forward.

Generosity is shown not just in financial exchanges. You can behave generously by listening well and often to employees, providing stretch assignments to junior workers, and assuming positive intent when someone makes a mistake.

This is the fruit of generosity. Recipients tend to give it back and pay it forward.

When a team member knocks on your door and asks a question, are you generous with your time and attention, by turning toward the person, focusing on their question and providing direction? Or do you continue to answer emails while half-listening to the employee?

I once had a boss who, whenever I knocked on her door, insisted on moving out from behind her desk where her computer was, and meeting me at her small conference table. She not only walked away from distractions but also demonstrated her full attention to me by asking powerful questions that helped me figure out what to do.

That kind of generosity costs nothing but pays huge dividends in the form of engaged and loyal employees.

Resilience

When teaching a leadership seminar, I often ask participants to list the positive characteristics of their best boss. In the lists, there are always references to "calm," "positive," and "able to go with the flow." These adjectives sum up resilience, which is the ability to rebound after a setback in business.

Remember that all eyes are on you when you lead. Your team will take their cue from you on how to respond to bad news or a failure. Keeping this in mind, the self-aware manager will spin bad news so that team members do not bear the responsibility for the failure; rather, they can appreciate the lessons learned in the doing and apply it to future challenges.

Leadership Styles

Dr. Daniel Goleman, author of *Emotional Intelligence* and *Primal Leadership,* studied the leadership styles of hundreds of managers and distilled them into six distinct styles: Affiliative, Democratic, Commanding, Visionary, Pacesetting, and Coaching. Each leadership style has a distinct effect on the culture of a workgroup, ranging from highly positive to negative. And, there are appropriate times and places for each style. The savvy manager knows when to use each one, depending on the needs of the situation.

Consider each of these leadership styles as a tool in your toolbox. When faced with a leadership challenge, wisely choose which tool or approach to apply. As you read through these leadership styles, use the worksheet at the end of each section to think of some challenges you have faced, or have seen other leaders face, in the past. Decide which leadership style you used during that situation and analyze the results. Would you apply the same leadership tool in the future or choose a different one? I also invite you to think of a time when you've observed another leader using each style and to rate the results of that behavior.

The ability to choose the best leadership style for a challenge is what sets apart great leaders from the merely good. Teach yourself to be aware of the styles, to notice them in yourself and other managers, and when best to use them.

Affiliative

Each of the six leadership styles is a tool in your toolbox. Use them according to the needs of the challenge you face.

An affiliative leadership style is one that promotes harmony and positive relations with and among the team. A manager exercises this style when she gets to know each of her team members, their strengths, and weaknesses, what motivates them, what career ambitions they have, and what their family and social life is like.

Using an affiliative style, a leader might seek consensus on certain decisions, such as ones that are not critical to her authority and that could benefit from input from the team. This style is exemplified by a positive attitude, friendly demeanor, and high sociability between the leader and the team. A manager using this style promotes strong relationships with her team and among team members, perhaps by sponsoring regular team social events.

This style is best used in two situations. The first is when a team needs to heal due to trauma in the past. Although trauma is a strong word to apply to team experiences, teams and whole organizations can go through suffering and pain that is traumatic. Examples of distressing situations include a failure to meet a goal with very negative consequences, a reduction in force, a betrayal of trust, an abuse of power (either on the part of a boss or team member), or a death.

The second situation to use an affiliative style is when you are leading a team of experts who are very good at their jobs. When you have a team of high achievers who have proven to you they do their jobs well, it is appropriate to occasionally employ an affiliative approach and be very friendly with your team members. Just remember to pull another leadership style out of your toolbox when you need to set the vision or discuss a performance issue. As my father, who was an exceptionally successful and beloved leader, used to remind me, "Familiarity breeds contempt."

I would soften his words by rephrasing his aphorism this way: "Don't try to be best friends with your team members. You are still their manager." When used in appropriate situations, this style results in a positive climate for the team.

Sally, a business unit manager for a high-tech company, excelled in building a team of high performers. She often used an affiliative style, by keeping an open door for all team members, sponsoring many team social events, laughing and joking with the staff, and generally keeping the tone of the office jovial. Working for her was fun because she molded a vibrant team. Sally would kick off her heels and run around the office in her stocking feet to tell the team some good news. At the same time, she knew when to pull out a commanding style when making hard personnel decisions, or a visionary style to set strategy for the year. The team was traumatized when she was replaced by a weak but commanding leader who used public humiliation as a motivational aid. (His style didn't work. All the good workers found other jobs and left the company.)

REFLECTION POINT:

When have you observed yourself or another leader using the affiliative style?

....

....

....

What was the situation in which you observed that person using this style?

....

....

....

Were the results of using this style positive or negative? Explain.

....

....

....

Democratic

The democratic style builds consensus among team members by inviting participation. Often, a leader using this style will seek input into decisions and will choose the alternative that most people support. Majority rules, so to speak.

This leadership style is helpful in situations in which you need to create buy-in or consensus, such as implementing a change that directly affects the group. It is also useful when you manage a group of trusted and expert workers, whose opinion and judgment you value.

To use the democratic style, you could convene a meeting to vet different solutions to a problem, or you could reach out to your team on an individual basis. Gathering input from your team before making a decision engenders a highly positive team atmosphere. Team members feel valued when their opinions and viewpoints are sought after and listened to. Remember, however, the process of gathering input takes time, so when a decision is needed urgently, this is not the most expedient style.

REFLECTION POINT:

When have you observed yourself or another leader using the democratic style?

....

....

....

What was the situation in which you observed that person using this style?

....

....

....

Were the results of using this style positive or negative? Explain.

....

....

Commanding

The commanding leadership style could also be called the "command and control" approach. This style is exemplified when a leader tells the team to "Do this, or else!" and then checks up on employees (micromanaging) to see that it is done.

This style represents a Theory Y approach to management that assumes workers dislike their tasks and are at a job only for the paycheck. Therefore, these employees must be closely monitored and controlled for best output (MacGregor 2006). Even though this style has deservedly enjoyed much notoriety in the twenty-first century, it is useful in the right context. When there is a crisis, a turnaround situation, or a problem employee, a manager must engage this style to get things done.

When an employee is on a performance improvement plan, there is little room for affiliative or democratic management. Likewise, in a crisis, everyone might lose their head and act accordingly. However, the prudent manager will remain calm, take control, and tell people what to do.

I once was an executive in a large call center when the fire alarm went off. There was a fire on a floor above us. Because my team was so devoted to customer care—and because there had been so many false alarms in this building—I had to go around to each cubicle and command, "There is a fire emergency. Hang up the phone and go to the staircase—now." This is an appropriate use of the commanding leadership style.

I once coached a high-level manager who was most comfortable with a commanding leadership style. As an illustration, he told his team, "I have three rules:

1. Keep your mouth shut.

2. Keep your head down.

3. Do your job."

This manager engendered a lot of respect because he was so technically brilliant and honest, but there wasn't a lot of happiness on his team. Interestingly, he was a tender-hearted man underneath the gruff exterior, but he seldom revealed that side of himself.

I encouraged him to loosen up his rules a bit, show some appreciation for his team, and start communicating more often. He could achieve a promotion because of his changed behavior and moved into a position much more suited to his personality and his talents.

When used to excess, the commanding style negatively affects the climate of a team. Millennials, that oft-maligned generation, will most often chafe under this management style, since they were not raised to blindly obey orders. They are more comfortable working under the other leadership styles, so employ this commanding style sparingly.

REFLECTION POINT:

When have you observed yourself or another leader using the commanding style?

....

....

....

What was the situation in which you observed that person using this style?

....

....

....

Were the results of using this style positive or negative? Explain.

....

....

....

Visionary

The visionary leadership style is shown to have a highly positive effect on a team's climate and productivity. When using this style, a leader will communicate the vision of a future state, inspiring people to contribute to its achievement. This style demands creativity, determination, and the ability to communicate effectively. Quiet leaders can be as visionary as extroverted ones. It only takes commitment to the cause and the ability to describe it to people in ways that evoke positive emotions.

Steve Jobs is often cited as the quintessential visionary leader. Yes, he disrupted multiple industries with his vision for easy-to-use, beautifully designed electronics, and galvanized his company to produce them under crushing deadlines but he also was a great leader. Do not despair, however, if you are not a Steve Jobs type of leader. He was charismatic but mercurial. I probably wouldn't have liked working for him. I prefer a leader who is true to her own personality, authentic in her emotions, passionate about the vision, and compellingly describes where the organization is headed.

When have you observed yourself or another leader using the visionary style?

....

....

....

What was the situation in which you observed that person using this style?

....

....

....

Were the results of using this style positive or negative? Explain.

....

....

....

Pacesetting

This leadership style is named after racing pacesetters, in both running and other sports, who set the speed for other contestants. In management, it is too often seen in new managers and managers who are unable to delegate effectively and inspire their teams to do good work.

The pacesetting leader sets high performance standards that only he can live up to. In fact, his definition of good work encompasses only the way he does it, with no deviations.

Often, it is the pacesetting leader who runs the race alone, leaving all others behind. This type of leadership negatively affects the climate of a team.

Here are some questions to ask yourself to determine whether you are overusing a pacesetting style:

- Am I the last one in the office most nights?

- Are my employees failing to live up to basic expectations of the job, spurring me to complete their assignments for them?

- Am I obsessed with doing everything better, achieving more and finishing tasks faster?

- Are my employees demoralized?

- Are my employees dragging down the overall performance of the team?

If you have said yes to three or more of these questions, you may be exercising a pacesetting style too often.

Learn to delegate well by setting clear but reasonable goals and expectations. Trust people to do a good job. Check in with employees at reasonable time intervals.

Allow—no, *expect*—them to complete tasks differently than you might. Go home at a reasonable time. Tell yourself, "There is always another day."

REFLECTION POINT:

When have you observed yourself or another leader using the pacesetting style?

....

....

....

What was the situation in which you observed that person using this style?

....

....

....

Were the results of using this style positive or negative? Explain.

....

....

....

Coaching

The coaching manager is a hot topic in leadership circles today. It is an antidote to the commanding leadership style that expects people simply to do what you tell them to. Instead, leaders using this style assume that employees are "naturally creative, resourceful, and whole" (Kimsey-House et al., 2011) and can therefore find solutions with just a bit of encouragement through skillful questioning.

In the spirit of collaboration, a coaching leader asks each team member what they have tried and/or have considered to-date. Together, they brainstorm other solutions, and, if necessary, the manager suggests an alternative one.

Leaders can take on a different role and persona when they coach. Setting aside their focus on team metrics and achievements, they turn their attention solely toward the employee. They consciously reserve judgment and become receptive to listening deeply and appreciatively to the team member.

To best apply this coaching style, it is important to symbolically set aside a certain time to do so.

The best coaching managers will schedule and designate time to coach their team members and will use symbols, such as selecting a clipboard for note taking (like a sports coach would), to designate their time set aside to be coach.

REFLECTION POINT:

When have you observed yourself or another leader using the pacesetting style?

....

....

....

What was the situation in which you observed that person using this style?

....

....

....

Were the results of using this style positive or negative? Explain.

....

....

....

Ego Development, Mindfulness, and Stress

As recently as fifty years ago, scientists thought that at age twenty-five, the human brain contained all the neurons it was ever going to have. Therefore, student doctors were told in the 1960s to curtail their drinking habits because alcohol consumption can kill brain cells, and once they are gone, they are gone. The good news of recent neuroscientific research is this: Neurogenesis, or the action of creating new brain cells, continues in the brain until a human being dies. What's important about this for leaders is that adults not only continue to create new brain cells for their entire life but also build more and more complex connections between them, enabling improved thinking skills and personal maturity.

> **Adults not only continue to create new brain cells throughout life but also mature through stages of development.**

Once science discovered the adult's ability to continue to learn into old age, researchers started noticing that adults, like children, go through stages of ego development, and there is a sequence of developmental stages. Adults proceed from lower forms of concrete thinking to more abstract thinking and broader perspectives. There are many theories and models about adult stages of development, including systems such as Spiral Dynamics by Beck and Cowan (1996), Action Inquiry by Torbert and Cook-Greuter (2006) among others.

A leader demonstrates later stages of adult development by exercising the following characteristics:

- A holistic business vision that includes profit, people, and planet (the three Ps)

- A deep sense of purpose, beyond making a profit

- The exercise of power in a collaborative, not punitive, manner

- The ability to see multiple options and approaches to problem solving

- The ability to hold paradox in mind, also called "both/and" (as opposed to "either/or") thinking

- The ability to balance short- and long-term objectives

- Emotional mastery, including both managing your own feelings and managing the mood of others to positive outcome

- Being present in the moment

- Seeking feedback to increase your self-knowledge

- The ability and desire to develop others and their teams

Leadership is not something that you turn on when you enter the office and turn off when you leave in the evening. The effectiveness of the leader reflects the character and maturity of the person. In fact, researchers have found a correlation between the attainment of later stages of ego development and the ability to successfully lead businesses through periods of change and transformation.

Cindy Wigglesworth of Deep Change, Inc. has evangelized the concepts of spiritual intelligence. She defines spiritual intelligence as "the ability to behave with wisdom and compassion while maintaining inner and outer peace, regardless of the situation" (2012, 8). In other words, a spiritually intelligent leader can keep calm amid chaos, acting wisely and compassionately in the situation.

Wigglesworth describes twenty-one skills to learn in building what she calls Spiritual Intelligence or SQ. And, she has shown a correlation between higher levels of SQ and higher stages of ego development. Therefore, higher levels of SQ are also correlated with the ability to lead during periods of uncertainty, complexity and change.

Benefits of Meditation and Prayer

What helps leaders advance to later stages of adult ego development? Studies have shown that mindfulness practices such as meditation, prayer, taking time for self-reflection and being present to everyday situations are the best enablers of ego development. Leaders who tend to their inner life tend to operate at later stages of emotional and spiritual maturity, have a broader, more long-term world view, and operate effectively in a complex business environment.

Mindfulness practices have many other benefits:

- Increased ability to concentrate

- Reduced stress

- Increased empathy

- Reduced reactivity

- Improved mood and increased positive emotions

Dr. Paul Ekman, a neuroscientist and researcher at University of California San Francisco, tested the ability of long-time meditators to be non-reactive to what would normally be considered a very stressful situation. He brought into his laboratory a Buddhist monk who had practiced meditation daily for decades, connected him to brain scanning machines and gave him headphones to listen to music for the experiment. At a random moment, he played a recording of a loud gunshot in his headphones. The monk did not startle, as compared to a marked startle reaction measured in all participants in the control group (Levenson et al. 2016). While most of us do not encounter loud gunshot noises in daily life, this experiment demonstrates the calm that can be developed by those who practice mindfulness. Indeed, neuroscience has established that meditation quiets the neurological circuits that trigger fear and anger. Recognizing these benefits, companies such as Google and General Mills offer classes in mindfulness for their employees.

A Daily Habit

Fortunately, it isn't necessary to meditate for hours a day to enjoy the benefits of mindfulness practice. A daily practice of ten to fifteen minutes of meditation or prayer is enough to rewire and calm the brain. Joiner and Josephs, in their book, *Leadership Agility, (2007)* recommend following a forty-five-minute daily routine that is composed of the following activities:

- Fifteen minutes of aerobic exercise
- Fifteen minutes of meditation or prayer (they refer to it as "reflective awareness")

- Fifteen minutes for a review of the day and planning for the next day

A good way to ensure you get these activities completed is to build them into your daily schedule. Walking the dog, climbing the stairs to your office, or parking in the farthest spot from your building are easy ways to structure nature's best form of exercise (walking) into your day.

A good daily habit is to follow the 15/15/15 rule: 15 minutes of exercise, 15 minutes of mindfulness, and 15 minutes of review and planning.

Many executives meditate or pray in the morning before work, (remember, it takes only ten to fifteen minutes a day to produce beneficial results) and they schedule planning/review time into their work calendars.

Meditation focuses the mind on a repetitive action or phrase, such as the breath or a word such as "love" or "calm." While meditating, the mind often needs gentle reminders to refocus, as it will naturally wander.

There are many classes, books and online resources to help you learn to meditate or pray, so this book will not repeat any of those instructions. What is important is that you take time to do it. It's been said that the only bad meditation is the one you didn't do, so don't add any performance anxiety to just doing it.

You can structure your daily review and planning session in a few ways. Some people do their review at the end of the day and the planning in the morning. Others do both at night or in the morning.

One review technique is to examine the day just completed, perhaps hour by hour, and notice events that were satisfying or gratifying. I normally list three things in my journal that were highlights of the day. Also, I list one thing that I wish had gone better. I call that my "one to grow on."

Other people share their three highlights and one low light of the day with their partner before going to bed.

Regarding the planning session, you may wish to look at your calendar and notice the meetings you have scheduled and review your to-do list. List the three big things you want to accomplish that day.

I like to write them down in my journal or in my calendar so I can check items off as I accomplish them. Then, mentally prepare for the day's meetings.

Ask yourself these questions:

- What role do I wish to play in this meeting?
- What do we need to accomplish?
- What do these people need from me?
- How can I contribute to a successful meeting?

If you anticipate a stressful encounter that day, take a moment to mentally rehearse what might transpire and what the "best you" would say and do to remain calm.

By reviewing and planning your days, you will increase your mindfulness, reduce reactive behaviors, and walk through your day with intentionality. You'll soon find that you feel calmer and more relaxed as you follow this daily habit.

Leadership Examples from Case Study Companies

At all the company meetings I observed, the CEO actively participated in running the meeting. The leader's activities in the meetings ranged from teaching, inspiring, encouraging/praising, and correcting poor behavior to simply keeping to the agenda.

The leader's role in ensuring that corrections are presented in a positive light was underscored at Alkali, where one focus group participant said:

"We always start off {the Team Growth meeting} with positive or exciting news; it sets the tone. The owners want that tone for us and for our clients. Staying positive is important. There might be some corrections, but it still has that tone of positivity. It's night and day from other companies.".

As an example of inspiration at Alkali, the CEO Steven Neuner gives a talk every month called "Steve Speaks." He often uses the time to teach what he has learned at a conference or from a book he's read. At the meeting I observed, he reviewed the ten best habits of the company. For the first habit, the CEO solicited input from the President and then asked other employees to comment on how they see the other habits practiced at the company.

When speaking about the leader's influence with employees and how the leader can step into a pivotal role of shaping the corporate culture, Paul Spiegelman, former CEO of BerylHealth, remarked:

> "If you want to be a leader, you have to get out of your office. I am a certified introvert and don't like to be the center of attention, but we know the impact we can make."

Taking on the mantle of an executive leader is to assume the responsibilities of both spokesperson and role model for the culture.

At Marketwave, CEO Tina Young remarked that she spent her time on three things:

> "My focus is vision, culture, and talent. I have to cast the vision for the culture, but others must protect it."

Young understands that her role is to define the vision and the culture, while at the same time empowering her employees, especially her leadership team, to protect and nurture the culture. In this capacity, she tasked her administrative assistant with scheduling regular all-hands meetings, social events, and community service events. To her leadership team, she delegated internal processes, project management and direct employee supervision.

At Alkali, employees described their CEO as "charismatic" and "inspirational," and with "the heart of a teacher."

One concern that arises from observing the strong personality of a founder is the ability of the rest of the leadership team to carry on the culture when the company grows and the leader's attention moves from an inward focus on the employees, to an outward focus as the ambassador and chief spokesperson of the company.

As Richard Barrett observed, "Enlightened leaders...must build a values-driven corporate culture that is independent of their identity" (1998, 15).

This is a concern at Alkali, expressed by a focus group participant:

"As we get bigger, there might be a lack of access to Steve; you might not be able to bump into Steve. That's already changed—my access to Steve is less than before. It was Steve's enthusiasm and excitement that drew me to the company. [His enthusiasm] was like gas to fill up your gas tank."

At a company like this, they might be careful to build up the middle managers' ability to carry and nurture the values of the culture. Also, companies might create structures and programs that embed, maintain, and publicize the values, such as people programs, rewards and recognition, hiring and firing practices.

Key Concepts

1. To influence the rest of the company, leaders must be values-based exemplars for Happy Mondays. To do that, they must adopt a servant leader's mind and demonstrate the following qualities:

- Self-awareness

- Gratitude

- Empathy

- Trust/trustworthiness

- Humility

- Generosity

- Resilience

2. There are many styles a leader can assume during daily activities. Six styles we notice are: Affiliative, Democratic, Commanding, Visionary, Pacesetting, and Coaching. Know when to use each of these styles to best handle particular situations.

3. The adult brain continues to grow and learn new things until death. Adult development has been categorized into stages, with the later stages demonstrating broader thinking, more compassion, and the ability to hold paradox in mind. Leaders who demonstrate later stages of

ego development are more effective in business environments of change, complexity, and transformation.

4. Mindfulness practices and taking time for self-reflection are the most powerful engines of the adult ego development. Leaders who make a daily habit of meditation, prayer and examination become better bosses quicker.

5. Ensure the visibility of the leader in all-hands meetings. Roles that the leader might assume in these meetings include teaching, inspiring, encouraging/praising, correcting poor behavior and simply keeping to the agenda.

6. Employees view the CEO as inspiring if he or she publicly corrects organizational behavior in a manner that is positive and educational.

7. Even introverted CEOs must take on the responsibilities of being inspirational, visible, and outspoken for the company. All leaders are role models of the cultural values.

8. The CEO or leader is responsible for setting the vision, culture, and talent management, or ensuring that the right people are in the right seats on the bus. Leaders must delegate everything else.

9. A leader must repeatedly ask for feedback to avoid the "ivory tower syndrome" of management, in which the executive is

insulated from feedback and bad news. The leader must also monitor his reaction to feedback and express gratitude to the giver. It's OK to disagree with the feedback, but the leader must reward the courage of the person who provided it to encourage others to do the same.

10.   By developing middle managers and a pipeline of strong future leaders, the CEO can prevent the culture from becoming dependent on either his personality or presence. As a company grows, the CEO must allocate a significant portion of his energy to talent acquisition and development to perpetuate the culture, ensuring the future of the company.

Case Study Interlude: Alkali Insurance

Building Great People Practices

Alkali Insurance is a benefits and insurance brokerage group dedicated to changing the way both personal and business insurances are brokered in the United States. Alkali has created several processes that together are labeled the Empowered Advantage ™ program.

This program ensures that individuals and businesses get the lowest cost and highest coverage insurance with high touch service from the agency. Important to their culture is their Success Optimizer ™ program in which the company automatically rebids insurance contracts at their annual renewal date, ensuring the customer continues to get the lowest cost and highest value coverage.

The Success Optimizer often results in lower commissions to Alkali's team members but ensures customer long-time loyalty. Therefore, the company recognizes a sales person when he or she saves money for a customer upon insurance renewal.

Culture is important to Alkali because it differentiates them from the competition and ensures that the Empowered Advantage ™ program, which is counter-cultural for the insurance industry, works and is perpetuated in their organization.

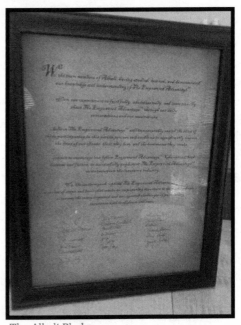

The Alkali Pledge

I observed both a weekly all-hands standing meeting, held every Monday morning for fifteen minutes, and a Team Growth meeting, which is held monthly for an hour. I also held focus groups and conducted executive interviews to gather data at this company. A noteworthy ritual at Alkali Insurance is an element of the company's onboarding and training program for new hires.

When new employees complete the ninety-day training period successfully, the company takes them to a local dinner theatre called Medieval Times, where they are ceremonially "knighted" and sign the Alkali pledge, seen above.

The pledge, which lists the guiding principles and behaviors of the company and has been signed by all Alkali employees for the last ten years, is mounted on the wall at the front door of the office.

This company does not have espoused values per se but has identified ten best habits, which include values statements in them such as commitment to integrity. In the Team Growth meeting that I observed, the CEO went over the ten habits and asked people to talk about what the habits mean and how they are embodied in daily work life.

CHAPTER 6

People Practices

If a culture is based on core values, what better place to embed those values than in the people practices you follow in your organization? If you don't embed them in everything you do, your core values will devolve into just a pretty plaque on the wall. What your company deserves are values that are lived and reinforced at every turn, so they become second nature to all employees. In this section, we explore how to weave the core values of your organization into all your people practices, so no one can forget them.

Performance Evaluations

Who doesn't dread their annual performance evaluation? Just the thought of it sends shivers down my spine, due to memories of being surprised and ambushed at worst and bored at best.

This section will introduce some innovative methods to make the performance evaluation more of a conversation that embeds the values of the organization and builds a positive relationship between the employee and manager.

There is great debate currently over whether an annual performance evaluation should be abolished. While the practice has its downfalls, we contend that there are several reasons to retain the practice in some form, including:

- Employees need to know where they stand in the eyes of management.

- To allocate annual merit increases, managers must rank their employees in some fashion. If the ranking is done outside of a formal evaluation process, it becomes non-transparent to team members. Without employees knowing where they stand, the practice risks being viewed as unfair and engendering distrust.

- Without a track record of poor performance reviews, it could be more difficult to terminate employees without legal repercussion.

- Annual ratings of team members add quantitative data for making promotion decisions.

We recommend embracing a more collegial, coaching approach to performance reviews rather than throwing out the annual performance assessment altogether.

As we shall see, there are ways to incorporate coaching into the annual rhythm of performance-related conversations and equip managers with appropriate skills to coach their employees successfully.

First, incorporate the core values into the performance evaluation form that you have. List the core values followed by the specific behaviors that each department devised in the core values exercise, above. Using a scale of one to five, with one being never and five representing always, rate the employee on the frequency with which they exemplify each behavior. You might have a form that looks like this:

We recommend embracing a more collegial, coaching approach to performance reviews rather than throwing out the annual performance assessment altogether.

Performance Review

Team Member:			Date:
Manager:			

Core Values:	Behaviors that support:	Rating (1 to 5): (Frequency of observed behavior)
		1 = Never, 2 = Seldom, 3 = Sometimes, 4 = Often, 5 = Always
Excellence	1. Doing the best possible job for all clients	5
	2. Proofreading, preferably by a non-author, of every document we send out	4
	3. Continual learning: attending classes, reading books, seeking out new approaches	4
	4. Creating a brand image that connotes excellence	3
	5. Seeking ways to add value at all times	5
Compassion	1. Assuming positive intent with employees, vendors & clients	4
	2. Paying employees & vendor at or above market rates	4
	3. Getting to know employees, partners and clients as whole	5
	4. Let love guide decision-making	5
	5. Listening generously	4
Integrity	1. Communicating honestly and transparently	4
	2. Admitting a mistake when you recognize it	3
	3. Practicing financial prudence	5
	4. Doing what you commit to	4
Balance	1. Building spaciousness into daily schedule	5
	2. Setting an example of getting enough sleep, exercise, prayer/meditation, healthy food	4
	3. Setting aside time every day to do something fun	3
	4. Taking adequate vacations and trips	4
Making a difference	1. Serving the larger community through contributions of time, money and talents	5
	2. Incorporating spiritual practices such as mindfulness, spaciousness of time and compassion into daily work	3
	3. Leaving a legacy through books, changed organizations, improved careers	4
	4. Creating organizations that weren't there before	5
	5. Touching people in their hearts	4

Employee Performance Review

Now, the question is, who should rate the employee? Some companies ask only the manager to rate each worker; others use it as a team-wide evaluation, like a 360-degree assessment, asking each team member and peers to rate his/her colleagues on the value behaviors. For managers, it is important to get values-based feedback from the team on an annual basis. In addition, a complete 360-degree assessment every two years of all managers is a good idea.

The biggest mistake a leader can make is to tolerate behavior of key executives that doesn't uphold the core values.

What you do with the values-based data you gather during the annual performance review will make or break your culture. If someone does not score over a three (which means the person exemplifies the behaviors some of the time) on the values portion of the evaluation, corrective action must be taken. Most companies have a policy about progressive corrective action.

Typically, it starts with a documented conversation about the behavior that needs to change and escalates through various written forms of documentation that over a specified time will result in termination. Failure to live up to the values of the organization must be treated as seriously as failure to perform job-related duties. If not, you can kiss your values good-bye.

All too often I observe organizations where a highly successful employee egregiously violates the espoused values. This person could be a highly productive salesperson or even an executive who achieves his goals without fail.

The question to the leader of the organization is, do you want to jeopardize your culture by tolerating this person's behavior? By tolerating a failure to demonstrate the values from this otherwise successful employee, you are negating all the goodness you expected from the work you've done on your culture. In fact, the culture will be worse than if you hadn't ever defined values and behaviors, because employees will recognize them for what they are: a sham.

The values-based behavioral assessment must be extended to the founder or CEO of the company. If the top leader finds herself getting marks lower than a three on any of the values-based behaviors, she should consider hiring an executive coach to help her develop her self-knowledge, self-reflection, and self-control. As we've noted before, power tends to corrupt, and without checks and balances, it will corrupt absolutely.

A yearly check of the employees' perception of how the top executive lives the core values is vital to a healthy culture. It is also a gesture of humility, one of the seven most important leadership characteristics that we've discussed in this book.

In addition to an annual evaluation, managers should be encouraged to have at least monthly check-in meetings with each of their employees. One method that gives needed structure to those monthly conversations is called the Five Conversations Framework, created by Dr. Tim Baker (2013.)

Baker advocates each manager spend about fifteen minutes monthly with each team member, five months out of six. There are five conversation topics that are conducted sequentially with a month's reprieve in the sixth month. In a year's time, each topic is covered twice. The manager makes notes from each conversation, either in a personal file or in the company's Human Resource Information System. The five conversations are as follows:

Culture Review

In this conversation, the manager learns about the employee's job satisfaction, morale, and sense of the effectiveness of organizational communication. Key questions to ask are as follows:

- How would you rate your job satisfaction on a one to ten scale?

- How would you rate the morale of our team on a one to ten scale?

- How effective are the communications you receive from both me and the organization? What would make them better?

A manager is encouraged to ask follow-up questions that delve into the reasons for each rating.

Strengths and Talents

A positive characteristic of the Five Conversations Framework is its emphasis on strengths, not weaknesses. Current organizational research shows that it is far more productive for an employee to work in her strengths than to improve her weaknesses. A bonus to working in strengths is higher job satisfaction and employee engagement. The key questions are as follows:

- What do you see as your strengths and talents?

- How can those be used better in both your current and future positions with the company?

Opportunities for Growth

In this conversation, growth refers to improving performance and standards and is considered from both the organizational and the individual's point of view. Key questions are as follows:

- What opportunities does our team have for performance improvement?

- How can I assist you to improve your performance?

Learning and Development

This conversation is focused on the desires and ambitions of the individual employee. Some questions to include:

- What skills would you like to improve?

- What learning opportunities would you like to have?

Innovation and Continuous Learning

In this meeting, the manager focuses on learning what to do to improve the efficiency and effectiveness of the business. Questions included are as follows:

- How could you improve your own working efficiency?

- How could we increase the effectiveness of our team?

When implemented well, the Five Conversations Framework increases communication, trust, and the bond between employee and manager. Warning: like any performance system, this should be rolled out only with careful planning and thorough training for all managers. Without that, the approach could be perceived as very threatening to employees. The Five Conversations can be an addition to or instead of the traditional annual performance review. Your culture will determine what is best.

Hiring

Although the entire breadth of hiring best practices is outside of the scope of this book, what needs to be highlighted is how to incorporate core values into the hiring process.

There are several methods to assess the cultural fit between a candidate and your company. One way is to conduct a cultural screening interview, perhaps over the phone. Another technique is to include values-based questions in the standard questionnaire that your team uses to interview all candidates.

Whatever method you use, the cultural interview should be conducted early in the process and used as a pre-requisite for further interviews. If the candidate does not fit the culture, do not proceed with further interviews. The two easiest mistakes to make in people practices are to hire for expertise rather than cultural fit and to retain people who don't live up to the core values.

Have courage in both situations. Even if a candidate is otherwise perfect for the job and you **First look for a culture fit in recruiting new hires.** are desperate to fill the open position, do not hire someone who has a poor chance of fitting into the culture. Set your bar high at the beginning of the relationship, and then you won't have to deal with firing those who can't uphold the core values.

Good questions to ask in a hiring interview are generally behaviorally based, where you ask people to tell stories about what they did in the past. To create relevant questions, go back to your values and supporting behaviors worksheet. Review the behaviors that support each value, and devise questions that assess the behaviors.

Here are some questions you can use in your standard interviews to probe the candidate's alignment with your core values. Values are <u>underlined</u>.

1. Tell me about a time that you had <u>fun</u> in your job.

2. Recall an incident that would tell me how <u>trustworthy</u> you are. Please share it.

3. How have you built <u>trust</u> with coworkers in the past? Give me some examples.

4. How do you like to be held <u>accountable</u> to job expectations?

5. Has there ever been a time when you chose <u>excellence</u> over expediency or just getting it done? Tell me about that.

6. Was there ever a time when you were tempted to ignore a troubling situation, but you chose to get involved despite your misgivings? (<u>compassion</u>)

7. Was there ever a time when you chose to do the right thing even though it was inconvenient? (integrity)

A good practice is to create an interview form that all interviewers complete on each candidate. Include numerical ratings for each value question using a Likert scale of one to five, where one is poor and five is the best possible.

Provide room for comments also. An overall rating of the candidate is good to ask interviewers to assign at the end of the interview form, along with the question: "Do you recommend hiring this candidate (yes or no)?" Here is an example of an interview form:

Candidate: Andrea Montecalvo Position: Sales Representative II	Date of Interview:					
1=Unacceptable 2=Below Average 3=Average 4= Above Average 5= Outstanding						
Values-based Questions (Core value is underlined)	Evaluation					Comments
Tell me about a time that you had fun in your job.	1	2	3	4	5	
Recall an incident that would tell me how trustworthy you are. Please share it.	1	2	3	4	5	

How have you built <u>trust</u> with coworkers in the past? Give me some examples.	1	2	3	4	5	
How do you like to be held accountable to job expectations?	1	2	3	4	5	
Has there ever been a time when you chose <u>excellence</u> over expediency or just getting it done? Tell me about that.	1	2	3	4	5	
Was there ever a time when you were tempted to ignore a troubling situation, but you chose to get involved despite your misgivings? (<u>compassion</u>)	1	2	3	4	5	
Was there ever a time when you chose to do the right thing even though it was inconvenient? (<u>integrity</u>)	1	2	3	4	5	
Overall Rating	1	2	3	4	5	

Interview Evaluation Report

In companies that value teamwork, candidates are asked to meet with numerous people and perhaps even be interviewed by a panel of potential teammates.

Be careful, though, as you broaden the number and kind of employees who interview candidates. Anyone who participates in job interviews should be trained by your People Department or Human Resources to ensure they know what they legally can and cannot ask of an applicant.

Examples of illegal interview questions include ones having to do with marital status, age, and religion. In this litigious age, you can't afford to have an Equal Employment Opportunity Commission complaint, or a lawsuit filed against you because of perceived discriminatory interviews practices.

Firing

As mentioned above under the performance evaluation, it is very challenging to insist that otherwise star performers be held accountable to behaviors that uphold the core values. If you don't, however, your culture will suffer. Rank and file employees will know that you tolerate poor behavior of the stars, and they will know that the core values are just window dressing and inauthentic.

Tolerating poor behavior creates a toxic environment, and the higher the rank of the toxic and tolerated person, the more poisonous the effect will be.

It takes executive fortitude to fire star performers for non-compliance with the values and supporting behaviors.

If you rate each employee for values-based behaviors and insist that all managers have 360-degree assessments bi-yearly, you arm yourself with metrics that cannot be ignored.

Onboarding

All the companies I have worked with have created thoughtful new-hire training programs. What is important in the scope of this book is to discuss ways to introduce values to new employees in an engaging manner so they begin to understand the foundations of the company culture. Typically, the CEO is involved in new-hire training in speaking to the core values, the purpose, and vision of the company. Hearing fundamentals such as values, purpose, and vision from the CEO is a symbolic of how important these statements are to the company and to the new hire's future.

Recognition

Connect your recognition programs to company core values.

Recognition is one of the most powerful tools to grow and sustain a vibrant culture. When you connect all recognition programs to core values, you send an unambiguous message that behaviors that uphold the company values are expected and encouraged. Recognition of the behaviors that support and zero toleration for the behaviors that detract from the values are the fastest way to grow a sustainable company culture.

Management by exception, in which the manager communicates with the employee only when the employee makes a mistake, is outdated. It was never an effective management tactic and it has been tolerated for too long. Management by exception will not work when managing millennials, who will make up half the workforce by 2020. Transformational management, on the other hand, works very well with millennials. Per Bernard Bass (1985), the strategies of a transformational manager are setting a vision, encouragement, recognition, and rewards for good performance. This method may sound like the "everyone gets a trophy" syndrome that millennials have been accused of needing. To the contrary, any employee, regardless of his or her generation, thrives on positive feedback and encouragement.

In the companies we observed, there are many recognition programs, often tied to values. Recognition programs to consider include the following:

Peer-to-Peer Recognition

In this form of recognition, employees identify peers for extraordinary actions that exemplify the core values.

These awards are typically given to highlight activities and behaviors; in other words, leading measures. For instance, a team member might recognize a peer for staying late on a Friday evening to complete a customer order. Companies choose names for this award that evolve out of company history, such as the "Go-getters award," "Atta boy/Atta girl award," or the "A-list award." Here is a form you might use as a template for creating your own award:

Catch someone doing something right!

On this day, _____ , I caught _____ doing the following awesome deed: _____

_____

_____

This exemplified our value of _____
Signed: _____

Peer-to-Peer recognition form

At Alkali Insurance for instance, all paper recognition forms from the previous month are put in a bowl, and a winner of a gift card is drawn. To intensify the fun, they ask the winner to attempt to putt a "hole in one" on the office's artificial golfing green. If successful, the winner receives an additional gift card.

Manager to Employee Recognition

This reward, also tied to core values, is one in which the manager nominates team members for an award.

You might encourage managers to recognize results and outcomes (lagging measures), rather than activities.

For example, a manager might recognize a team for completing an important project, or a customer service team member for achieving a targeted customer loyalty metric. These are the achievements that propel the organization toward its goals. The Leadership Team of the company should ensure that this award is given out fairly and consistently.

Manager to Manager Recognition

This award is like the peer-to-peer recognition in that it is tied to values. Activities or results are appropriate at this level. The power of this award is that it encourages collegial teamwork and discourages competition between managers. When a manager is encouraged to identify the positive actions of his peers, there is less likelihood of an "us vs. them" attitude.

The Annual President's Award

The President's Award is given by the chief executive in honor of activities and results that exemplify core values.

At one company, candidates for this award are nominated by managers throughout the company once a year. Nominees are vetted by the Culture Committee (caps here? You didn't use caps before.) and a short list of finalists is presented to the Executive Leadership Team for final approval. They select one or more winners for the year's award. At a special all-hands ceremony, the winners of the award are announced with a video of their co-workers, family, and managers praising the recipient.

A significant prize is awarded and recipients' photos are hung on a "wall of fame" in the corporate office.

The values-based culture will institutionalize recognition, appreciation, and rewards into its people practices. Tying every reward back to the core values is the best way to embed the culture.

Key Concepts

1. To embed your culture in everything you do, all your People Practices must be based on the core values of the company, including performance evaluations, hiring, firing, onboarding, and rewards/recognition.

2. In addition to an annual performance evaluation, many companies are training their managers to conduct structured monthly conversations with employees. This approach is called the Five Conversations.

Case Study Interlude: Marketwave

Innovative Meeting Rituals

This marketing agency is comprised of eighteen professionals and led by CEO Tina Young. At this company, most of the staff members are millennials. Both the CEO and her husband work in the company. Here, I observed a monthly all-hands meeting, called the Victory Laps meeting, in which the CEO updated "Connecting to What Counts" metrics on an infographic drawn in chalk on a blackboard-painted wall.

Marketwave's Connecting to What Counts infographic

At the beginning of the year, all team members were given a journal with the "Connecting to What Counts" metrics listed on the inside front cover. Team members are expected to note their personal accomplishments in the journal and report them at the Victory Laps meeting. Metrics tracked are activities such as number of proposals sent, speaking engagements landed, new wins, awards won, etc. To show their love for animals, their last metric counts how many dogs the employees own. During this meeting, the team added a rabbit and a parakeet to the total, so now the metric is for total pets. Food was served at this meeting, and an informal collegial tone was set.

Marketwave has a tradition of creating vision boardss or vision boards at the beginning of the year. Marketwave frames the boards, which are eight-by-eleven inches large, and asks employees to display them at their desks.

Marketwave's wall plaques displaying core values

A noteworthy practice in this office is the prominent display of core values on the wall where everyone can see them. The values themselves were etched on Lucite plaques with lettering affixed to the wall underneath. These values underscore the culture and are recognized in the Victory Laps meetings each month.

CHAPTER 7

Rituals, Symbols, and Stories

This element of the *Company Culture Ecosystem* is the most difficult for many hard-charging, practical businesspeople to understand and commit to managing. To the practical mind, these topics might seem ephemeral or fluffy. To the contrary, rituals, symbols, and stories speak to the subconscious mind of your team members and can be the most powerful tool in cultivating the type of culture you desire. When you understand the leverage these elements provide you, you will soon be looking for ways to consciously build rituals, symbols, and stories into the life of your company.

Rituals are repetitious routines and ceremonies. Ideally, they should be constructed to evoke positive emotions and embed value-driven behaviors in organizations. Examples of rituals include new hire and retirement ceremonies, holiday parties, monthly lunches, and food that is served at regular times.

Not only can rituals embed corporate values, but they can both reduce anxiety and help employees make meaning of events. Goleman, Boyatzis, and McKee (2002, xi-xii) tell a story about an executive in New York City who helped his company create meaning after the events of 9/11, in which colleagues and family members of the company were killed. He spoke regularly to the company and addressed them nightly in emails meant to comfort them and direct their energy toward the good. This leader created a culture of emotional support and compassion for those grieving and channeled their emotions into a day of fund-raising for victims of the tragedy.

> **Symbols of your culture include your visual brand identity and colors, marketing products, the layout of your office, and the physical set-up for meetings.**

This chapter contains references to the studies I conducted of five companies in various industries to discover and understand the rituals used in meetings to embed company culture. What I found was a treasure chest of good practices that are shared in these pages.

While rituals are enactments, symbols are typically visual and physical. Symbols of your culture include your visual brand identity and colors, marketing products, the layout of your office, and the physical set-up for meetings. When they first walk into your company's offices, what will visitors see? Persian rugs and mahogany furniture will portray a different company culture than exposed concrete floors and second-hand furniture.

Be careful what stories you tell about your culture as they, more than any other verbalization, will impart the essence of your culture. When asked about how to promote the positive stories over any negative ones, a high-ranking culture officer of a large restaurant chain told me, "Just be careful which ones you repeat."

There will always be complainers in any culture; just don't give them any notice. Publicize the stories that paint the culture the way you want it to be perceived; work like heck to eliminate the cause of any negative ones you hear. What's even nicer is when your customers tell positive stories about your company.

That's what happened to Chili's, the restaurant chain, when a young customer with autism was served a "broken" cheeseburger. The staff had sliced her cheeseburger in half for easier handling, and to this young girl's perception, it was "broken." The waitress immediately ordered a new cheeseburger and ensured that it was not sliced. The older sister of the happy customer posted this outstanding customer service story on Facebook (MacLean 2013), which went viral. Talk about a positive company culture story!

Leaders can use the emotional power of a story to reinforce the positive aspects of the culture. Many executives make a point of telling stories about employees who exemplify the core values when they award recognition to an employee (see section on rewards and recognition). This powerful practice encourages other employees to do similarly virtuous actions and sets the standard for exemplary conduct in the company.

Meeting Rituals

Meetings have been referred to as the "most important management ritual" (Deal and Kennedy 2000) and therefore are worthy of any manager's attention. In our observations of companies with positive cultures, we notice that meeting rituals can be a powerful way to embed the values and culture of the company in themselves, so meetings were attractive to study ritual and to embed corporate culture.

We attended and observed regularly scheduled all-hands meetings at five companies known to have vibrant company cultures. In this section, we look at lessons learned about effective meeting rituals from these innovative companies.

Are Meeting Rituals just a Lot of Hoopla?

To the contrary, meeting rituals are vital to the health of one's company culture because they transmit the values and beliefs of an organization. Deal and Kennedy (2000) note that "behind each ritual is a myth that symbolizes a belief central to the culture of the organization."

It is therefore important for an organization to structure rituals with conscious intent about what beliefs or values they stand for. Rituals and ceremonies, whether they are large extravaganzas or simple events, are needed to "keep values, beliefs, and heroes uppermost in employee's minds and hearts" (Deal and Kennedy, 2000). Both individually and collectively, employees examine and deduce meaning in all rituals of corporate life. To take advantage of that tendency, leaders can consciously develop and nurture the communication rituals in their meetings.

Many of the meeting rituals I observed centered on recognition programs, particularly peer recognition. In two companies, there was a drawing for monthly winners of the peer recognition program.

Meeting rituals are vital to the health of the company culture because they transmit values and beliefs of the organization.

In both cases, paper certificates were completed by employees to praise coworkers for their efforts and results. The certificates were put in a large bowl and one was drawn to identify the winner.

At both companies, a gift card for $10 was the prize, indicating that the reward doesn't have to be a large dollar amount. At Marketwave, each of the fourteen attendees received recognition and appreciation during the Team Kudos section of the meeting agenda. At BKM

Total Office of Texas, the Vice President of Sales recognized employees that were mentioned by customers in satisfaction surveys or emails. At Acuity Systems, people were appreciated and encouraged as they shared their accomplishments.

At two of the large companies we studied, they practiced similar rituals of drawing a winner from all the submitted peer recognition awards since the last meeting. In the largest company, the recognition program was administered online, meaning that the form to recognize a co-worker was available via the company intranet. In both cases, the form included a field to show what core value the recognized employee was displaying. This important connection to the core values is a best practice for other companies.

Another ritual observed in the two companies was individual check-ins. The CEO of Alkali used a check-in ritual of asking each attendee to share something "positive and exciting" to start the monthly Team Growth meeting. In one instance, he skillfully guided an employee away from a complaint and back to the positive, signaling the inherent danger in this type of practice when used in larger groups.

At fifteen attendees, the Alkali meeting is almost too large to include a check-in because it carries a risk of taking up too much time. The meeting I observed at Share on Purpose was attended by only three people, and the inclusion of a check-in was appropriate and successful in setting the tone for the meeting. At this meeting, the leader asked each attendee to articulate something she was grateful for in the previous week.

A ritual of check-in, when it includes both professional and personal accomplishments, demonstrates the value the company places on overall well-being of the employee. Sharing personal information also builds relationships between the manager and employee and is an indicator of managerial effectiveness.

Plan a Meeting Cadence

To help you devise a meeting cadence that embeds your desired company culture, it helps to set out a master plan. Your culture committee, along with the CEO, should intentionally design a schedule of weekly, monthly, quarterly, and annual meetings and consciously devise which values each is intended to uphold. You might use a spreadsheet to help you map your meetings, like this:

HAPPY MONDAYS

Frequency:	Attendees:	Purpose/ Agenda:	Ritual Description:	Food Served:	Values instilled:
Weekly meetings:					
1					
2					
3					
4					
Monthly meetings:					
1					
2					
3					
4					
Quarterly meetings:					
1					
2					
Semi- Annual meetings:					
1					
2					
Annual meetings:					
1					
2					
Annual social events:					
1					
2					
3					

Meeting Rituals: Key Concepts

1. Create rituals of recognition that tie positive behaviors to core values.

2. Consider implementing a peer recognition practice that encourages teamwork and appreciation among employees.

3. Consider implementing a drawing for a small prize from the peer recognition forms that were submitted since the last large group meeting.

4. Be sure to have the leader (CEO or Department head) publicly award the recognition, by conducting the drawing (if that is your practice), presenting the award, and verbally thanking the employee for their contribution to upholding the company values.

5. For smaller meetings, consider implementing a check-in ritual in which each attendee shares something positive from either their professional or personal life. This practice bonds the group and creates an open and caring relationship between the manager and employees.

Food Rituals in Organizations

Research on company food rituals offers a less-frequently-found perspective on organizational culture. Lessons learned from our studies are important for all leaders to understand to devise meaningful food rituals that advance your culture and embed positive values in your employees.

A basic tenet of human sociability is commensality, which simply means eating and drinking together around a table (Fischler 2011, 529). Commensality creates group belongingness and, perhaps more importantly, delineates who is excluded from the group (Fischler 2011, 530; Julier 2013, 187; Plester 2014, 254). A positive aspect of working for a company is the sense of belonging it provides to employees (Schein 2010, 304). Recognizing this human need, companies might consider providing metaphorical vehicles, such as a shared meal or serving a special food, to enhance a sense of belonging.

Eating together creates a sense of belonging to the group.

Food rituals are extremely common in the workplace and in meetings. In fact, Professor Michaela Driver listed twenty-two different organizational events that include serving food (2008, 917), including parties, recognition celebrations, picnics, luncheons, training sessions, and CEO talks. These events were discovered in her interviews of thirty-five research participants from different organizations.

Driver notes that the serving of food can be used by management as a reward to employees for a job well done or as a celebration of goal achievement. Driver reports that employees associate food served by management with positive emotions: participants in her study reported that food is "comforting," "associated with love and joy," and makes people "happy."

Food rituals reinforce organizational culture and infuse meaning into business activities (Cabral-Cardoso and Cunha 2003, 371–79). Professor Barbara Plester studied food rituals in organizations and discovered that eating structures social events and sharing food incorporates the partaker in the community (2014, 251–68). This is important because building a feeling of belonging or community increases employee loyalty and engagement.

Furthermore, Professor Plester found that, in food rituals, the participant ingests food provided by company management and makes it a part of his/her body. Because the meal is typically paid for by management, the food becomes a de facto symbol of the company.

Plester found that ingesting food from the company transfers the perceived values of the ritual to the self and influences employees' perceptions of the organizational culture. Her research suggests that ingesting company-provided food and drink may be a powerful way to assimilate people into the company culture (2014).

Several researchers warn managers against using food rituals to coerce employees into behavior compliant with their expectations. Organizations should be concerned that offering food, because it is such a primal act, is controlling or patriarchal (Plester 2014, 266).

Driver cautions that food gifting from an employer "may be seen as having exchange value" in the sense that food could be a reward or bribe for good behavior, but also notes that food could be used an incentive for attending meetings, events, or training sessions (2008, 919).

In this and other ways, commensality is not "devoid of any risk or pain." There is the physical risk of eating tainted food that might cause illness, especially if the meal is home cooked. There is also a potential perceived risk inherent in fraternizing with people lower in the hierarchy (Fischler 2011, 538).

Executives and managers might be loath to break down the barriers between them and the employees if they are concerned about wielding an element of positional power (Thomson and Hassenkamp 2008, 1792).

Food Rituals in Example Companies

I had the privilege of working as a consultant with the Senior Vice President (SVP) of a global, three-hundred-member department of a large, multi-national firm. This SVP was committed to creating a culture of respect, opportunity, accountability and positive communications, and he and I worked closely together to accomplish that. At that organization, food was a common element of meetings and off-sites. The SVP's quarterly webinar-based meeting with his global workforce was entitled "The Cookie Chat" because he insisted that the administrative assistants in each location purchase and serve cookies for the local employees during this meeting (Stegner, 2015). He regularly served food and often complete meals at his leadership team meetings. Stegner understood the power of serving food provided by the company. It drew his team together and created a family-like atmosphere.

Food is the universal language. It unites us.

At Marketwave, food was shared at the Victory Laps meeting by passing bowls of snacks among the participants. Finger foods such as chocolates and apple chips were in the bowls, and nonalcoholic drinks were available in the kitchen. The menu at Share on Purpose's Purpose Party included nachos and drinks of one's choice at a restaurant/bar near the office.

At the Share on Purpose's Purpose Party, the conversation was light-hearted and casual. CEO, Terri Maxwell, had described the party as follows:

"Attendance is not required, it's just social. It's an opportunity for us to break bread together, to get to know each other. There might be 25 people, or 5 or 6 there. We try different things each month. And when we are clicking along, there are more people there. It's an indication that something's not right if people don't show up. It allows me to take the temperature of the company and the portfolios within it."

When asked about the subject of food served at meetings, most employees were enthusiastic and positive about its effect on them. "Food is the universal language. It unites us," said one employee at Alkali.

At BKM, when I asked employees about the possibility of providing food at its quarterly meeting, employees thought it would allow participants to linger over the food, converse, and create a bond while sharing food. (Julier 2013). One employee remarked, "Even a box of doughnuts shoved on the counter would represent nurturing." Her observation about nurturing confirms the research of Driver, who found that food served by the organization is a symbol of warmth and caring (2008).

Company leaders must balance, on the one hand, the knowledge that the type of food served to employees represents the values of the company; on the other hand, the strong benefits of serving food of any type, even junk food, at a meeting. Especially if the leaders want to appear more caring and warmer to their employees, serving food is an excellent choice.

All the companies we studied described rituals at social events that included food and drink. At Acuity Systems, the owners invited employees to their homes for drinks before going to a company dinner at a restaurant. The employees had noted that social events had yet to be consistently scheduled despite the company's intention to host such events every month. With the recent hire of an administrative assistant to coordinate culture activities, the group hoped that the dinners would be scheduled and implemented more regularly, something that was important to the team members.

Another company mentioned sharing food and/or drinks at their CEO's home. At Succeed on Purpose, employees fondly remembered company dinners at the home of the founder, Terri Maxwell. She discontinued that practice when the company grew too large for her house. It seems that opening the home of the founder or CEO is impactful on employees. Like other food rituals, being served a meal in the CEO's home appears to break down barriers and build intimacy among employees and managers, resulting in higher engagement, loyalty, and productivity of the employees.

Small Organizations, Take Heart: The Value of the Potluck

In contrast to food served by the company or management, which is a symbol of the organization's warmth and caring (Driver 2008). Alice Julier examines in-depth the meaning and outcomes of a potluck meal served in a home among non-kin people (2013). Parallels can be drawn to potluck meals at the workplace, which are common in companies (Driver 2008, 917) because of the potluck's low cost to the organization of providing food.

The research shows that smaller organizations, whether it's a whole company or a department within a larger corporation, can benefit from potluck meals. This is good news because many smaller organizations may not have the budget to provide full meals to their employees on a regular basis.

Fortunately, Julier identifies the meanings and positive outcomes of a potluck meal. In her book, *Eating Together: Food, Friendship and Inequality* (2013, 157), she describes how these egalitarian meals tend to level the social hierarchy in a group. The cost, the social responsibility, and the preparation of a potluck meal is shared equally across all levels of the organization. No one, including management, assumes the responsibility of providing all the food.

This type of meal offers a temporary suspension of social inequalities, hierarchies, and differences and ultimately creates a bond between all partakers. At Alkali, for example, the company plans a monthly potluck lunch at which the company provides only the meat and the birthday cake for employees; everything else is provided by employees.

Some companies plan annual chili cook-offs, a form of a competitive potluck in which eaters vote on their favorite chili dish. The winning cook is celebrated with applause and a recognition form. Other companies conduct guacamole cook-offs, insisting that the "guac" is made on site with real ingredients. As with a chili cook-off, partakers vote on the best-tasting dish, and the winning cook is celebrated.

One variation on the potluck is described by Thomson and Hassenkamp (2008, 1784–1786). Every Friday was "cake day" at the health-care clinic they studied. A rotating member of the health-care team was responsible for bringing in high-quality cakes for the group. Cake day was a reward for hard work and provided a food ritual that minimized the hierarchal gaps in the group and strengthened social bonds.

The Role of Alcohol in Meeting Rituals

Julier cites alcohol as a "social lubricant for intimacy" (2013, 76). She goes on to say that serving alcohol creates an intimacy that is not present at another meal or event.

Imbibing alcohol, with its anti-inhibitory effects, can break down social barriers at a company event. Alcohol tends to 1) relax people, 2) act as a social lubricant, and 3) soften the inherent hierarchy in an organization (Valentine 2002, 12; Julier 2013, 76). All these benefits have been shown to increase productivity and employee engagement.

Thus, serving alcohol is a way to increase bonds of intimacy between attendees. Because alcohol produces a pleasant effect and because food and drink served by a company become an ingested symbol of the company's culture (Plester 2014), alcohol could be an effective vehicle to help build a culture of teamwork and collaboration.

Imbibing alcohol, with its anti-inhibitory effects, can break down social barriers at a company event.

Although serving alcohol can result in breaking down hierarchies, creating a bond of intimacy among team members, it is important to set guidelines on appropriate use in your culture.

Caution! Be mindful of the legal responsibility of the company when employees drive while under the influence of alcohol.

Many companies will either appoint designated drivers, pay for taxis or Uber drivers, or buy a block of hotel rooms for use after a company holiday party, for example.

The behavior of the leadership team at these parties will set the standard of conduct for other employees, so be sure to brief your executives on limiting their alcohol consumption at company parties.

Here are some ideas to consider in creating guidelines that limit the possible adverse effects of serving alcohol at a company event:

- Communicate to your leadership team that their conduct sets the example for responsible drinking within the company. This is the most important guideline of all.

- Always provide nonalcoholic drinks and food alongside alcoholic beverages at a company event.

- Designate a bartender to serve drinks rather than offering an unlimited supply of self-served alcohol. Consider issuing a limited number of drink tickets to each team member.

- Provide alternative means of transportation to employees after major company events at which alcohol is served. Depending on your culture, that might mean arranging for discount tokens for taxis or Uber-type rides or encouraging each workgroup to identify a "designated driver." After major parties like a holiday party, some companies provide discounted hotel rooms for

Create guidelines for company events in which alcohol is served.

partygoers to ensure their safety at the end of the night.

- Require the practice of putting one manager in charge of each event at which alcohol is served. That person is responsible for monitoring the intoxication level of employees and helping them when necessary.

- Ensure that all employees understand that drinking is a choice, not a requirement, at any company event.

- Communicate that all employees are expected to uphold professional standards of conduct and behave in accordance with the law. For example, alcohol should not be served to minors.

Food Rituals: Key Concepts

1. Serving food can break down hierarchies and build closer relationships among a company's staff, resulting in higher productivity. Food is a symbol of caring for and nurturing your employees.

2. The food you serve will be subliminally viewed as symbolic of your company's cultural values. Employees who ingest these symbols are more likely to embody the values.

3. Carefully choose the food you serve, being conscious of the symbolism of the type of food served. Make sure you serve food that is emblematic of your culture. For example, if you are a wealth management firm that caters only to high net worth individuals, you probably don't want to have a messy potluck in the office, in case someone might drop spaghetti on the Persian rugs! On the other hand, if you are a scrappy, competitive and growing company that is focused on changing an industry, throwing a box of doughnuts on the counter might be just the right symbol for the cultural values you wish to embed.

4. Consider potluck meals when you want to create an egalitarian culture that celebrates the contribution of each person or when you can't afford to provide catered meals. Potlucks are

beneficial in valuing diversity of the employees when you encourage people to prepare dishes from their heritage.

5. Serving alcohol at company parties can relax people, act as a social lubricant, and break down the inherent hierarchy in an organization.

6. Be sure to provide appropriate care for inebriated employees after a gala event such as a holiday party. Ensure the leadership team models appropriate behavior regarding alcohol consumption at all events.

Room Configuration

The room configuration of a meeting space is a good clue to the culture of the company. At BKM Total Office of Texas, the room was set up for formal presentations, with the presenters in front and the "audience" of employees sitting auditorium style in back. Of all the companies observed, this was the most formal company culture.

Marketwave, on the other hand, chose to hold their meetings in an open area with couches, tables, and colorful ottomans set up in a semicircle around the chalkboard, making it seem more like a living room. Food was passed from person to person in a party-like manner. Marketwave, like BKM, uses its office as a marketing brochure and has consciously designed its space to reflect the innovation and fashionable marketing designs that it creates for its customers.

At Alkali, the meeting room's configuration gave clues to this company's culture also; the conference room table was purchased second- hand, and the

A meeting room's configuration is a symbol of your culture.

company had already outgrown the size of the conference room. In addition, the office space was clean, neat, and practical but not overly attractive in an unusual way. This indicates that the company is frugal in its expenditures, ensuring adequate but not extravagant office space. Alkali is an insurance company that prides itself on saving money for its customers, so an expensive or elegant office would be dissonant to the company's purpose.

At Acuity Systems, the culture is sales- and process-oriented. The training room is large, colorful, and spacious, but the staff meeting took place at the round conference table in the CEO's office. The round table physically represented the egalitarian nature of this company where everyone's opinions are valued, and all team members are accountable for the firm's success. This configuration encouraged participants to share their progress and challenges and to seek help from others when needed. Likewise, at Share on Purpose, the round tables are adequate but not elaborate, office décor was symbolic of the company's entrepreneurial yet nurturing culture.

Room Configuration: Key Concepts

1. Be conscious of the implicit cultural messages that your meeting room configuration delivers. Make sure that the space is reflective of, and not dissonant to, the company's cultural values.

   o For example, consider the differences between conducting a standing meeting, a meeting configured in auditorium style, or inviting people to gather around a table. If collaboration, for example, is one of your core values, how can you embody that value in your meeting space? Conversely, if formality and hierarchy are important values to your company, consider configuring your meeting room in a way that reflects that formality.

2. The room configuration also impacts the communication style that can be used in the meeting. Our observations suggest that round tables and more casual settings, like a typical living room, will encourage more interactivity and involvement. Conversely, a formal seating arrangement will be reflected in the behavior of the participants.

Use of Time

At all the observed meetings, there was a standard agenda structure that was unvarying for long stretches of time. At each company, what varied was the content of the various sections of the meeting, but the structure remained constant. The discipline of holding regularly scheduled meetings with a standard, nonvarying agenda is an important implication for practice.

In comparison with a flexible attitude toward time in many other countries, in the West we have "a strict sense of punctuality." (Kemp and Williams 2013, 215–35). Therefore, the start and end times of a meeting can be important indicators of the culture of the company.

At Acuity Systems, the staff meeting started whenever the customers left the office after the morning training classes. The meeting ended abruptly when the CEO and a salesperson had to leave to make a sales visit. This time elasticity might be perceived as disrespectful or undisciplined, or it could signal the importance of the customers to the business. At Acuity Systems, it was a common practice and appeared to reflect a focus on the customer rather than disrespect for the employees.

Keeping to stated frequency of meetings is also indicative of the culture. If a company says the all-hands meeting will be held every month, there is an implicit message regarding the importance—or lack thereof—of the meeting if a month is skipped or postponed.

At the other companies studied, the culture champion was instrumental in ensuring the consistent scheduling of all-hands meetings.

Use of Time: Key Concepts

1. Sticking to a standard and consistent meeting agenda is a ritual. Rather than contributing to boredom, the discipline of a standard agenda allows flexibility in content while providing the comfort of a consistent experience.

2. Create a company-wide schedule of meetings that cascade from infrequent, all-hands meetings to daily huddles of small work teams. Ensure that all managers hold meetings per this schedule.

3. Once a schedule of meetings is established, appoint someone like the culture champion or the CEO's administrator to ensure the meetings are held like clockwork, as promised to employees. The lack of follow-through and consistency in holding to a company meeting schedule could be perceived by employees to indicate that management doesn't care about them.

Sidebar Conversation: Vibrant Cultures

*Building a Vibrant Culture
Is More than Throwing a Great Party*

The holiday season is typically the time to throw a company party and many companies make a special effort for this annual ritual. While I love a party as much as anyone else, I caution business leaders to balance the attention and funds spent on parties with more day-to-day cultural issues. It's the daily experience that shapes your employees', customers' and suppliers' perception of the company. And yet, as we will see, there are plenty of good reasons to throw a fun party in December.

The following are practices that can negate all the fun and goodwill generated at your holiday party. You might use it as a checklist to make sure you aren't sabotaging your intentions:

Do you pay all your employees at market (or better) wages? Is gender pay equity a consideration in your salary reviews?

Have you defined your cultural values and embedded the values into everything you do, from hiring/firing to operational processes? Do you have the courage to terminate people, including leaders and rainmakers, who don't exemplify the company's values?

Do your employees have the tools they need to do their jobs efficiently? Do they have fast-enough computers and up-to-date software plus the knowledge to use them efficiently?

Have you trained your leaders to listen to and respect their employees, incorporate employees' ideas into the workflow, and empower them to solve problems within their jurisdiction?

Have you ensured that interdepartmental communications and workflow have been fine-tuned to create efficient and blame-free processes to get the work delivered?

Have you scheduled rituals outside of the holiday party that embed cultural values, such as recognizing employees who demonstrate behaviors that support values at monthly meetings?

Let's explore the good results that can be gained from a holiday party or other cross-functional social event at which food is served. Research demonstrates that sharing food together is a bonding experience. The word "commensality" describes the act of sharing food and drink around a table and has been shown to increase goodwill between people, to cement relationships and to incorporate the partaker into the community. Ultimately, commensality increases employee engagement, teamwork, and productivity. And, serving food increases the employees' perception of the company as caring and compassionate.

In conducting research into organizational behavior, Dr. Barbara Plester of the University of Auckland, New Zealand, discovered that, when an organization serves a meal to employees, the food becomes a symbol of the organizational culture. When employees ingest the food, they make it a part of their physical bodies. Plester shows that eating food transfers the perceived values of the company to the self and influences employee's perceptions of the organizational culture. Her research suggests that ingesting company-served food and drink may be a powerful way to assimilate people into the company culture. If the food is symbolic of the organization that offers it, employees become that organization when they eat it. The adage "You are what you eat" is pertinent in considering the importance of serving food at company events.

Here's good news for your holiday cheer: Both research and experience show that your holiday party is well worth the time, effort, and funds you put into it and can result in better teamwork, improved perception of the company, and greater productivity. The important thing to remember is that an annual event's impact will pale in comparison with your employees' day-in and day-out experience of the company. Pay attention to both and you will build a great company culture.

Case Study Interlude: Acuity Systems

Accountability Systems

Acuity Systems is a sales training and consulting company that is a franchisee of an international sales training program franchisor. Acuity Systems has sister companies in all major North American metropolitan areas, providing an opportunity for Acuity Systems employees to connect with an accountability partner who performs the same job at another franchisee. Besides the two owners of the company, who are admittedly five years from retirement, the rest of the employees are millennials, making for a young workforce.

I observed their weekly all-hands meeting in their office, sat in on their client training classes, interviewed the CEO, and ran a focus group.

Using windows to notate goals

What struck me most about this company is the discipline with which they run their company; they operate by consciously following the processes they teach in their sales classes; and they ensure that the company's seven values are posted on the door to each person's office.

A noteworthy visual ritual at Acuity Systems is writing quarterly goals with markers on the office windows. Because one doesn't expect to see windows used as walls, this practice commands a visitor's attention immediately. One employee remarked,

"By writing the goals on the windows, we watch out for each other's goals. Once, someone walked into my office and said, you haven't crossed anything off your goals recently."

These practices allow employees, and employers hold each other accountable to not only the company's goals but also individual ones, and the mutual support they foster helps to keep everyone on target.

HAPPY MONDAYS

CHAPTER 8

Operational Processes and Tools

You may think that operational processes and tools is an odd chapter to include in a book on company culture. To the contrary, the processes and tools that employees use daily can make or break your culture. Remember, company culture encompasses everything you do and that includes the daily tasks team members conduct and the tools they use. There are too many examples of companies that try to grow a vibrant culture but saddle their employees with inefficient processes and outdated tools to do their jobs, only creating a level of frustration that no amount of fun parties or compassionate managers can alleviate.

> Inefficient processes and out-of-date tools create a level of frustration that no amount of fun parties or compassionate managers can alleviate.

One Silicon Valley company that I worked for was like that. They sold a software product that had glitches and was unfit for its function, and the managers expected customer-facing employees to make the best of the situation. At the heart of the problem was an ineffective software development process that was undisciplined and unresponsive to market needs. In addition, interdepartmental processes were kludgy and pitted one group of employees against another.

For example, the salespeople were expected to sell software that wasn't yet market-ready, but the post-sales support people objected to selling "vaporware." And the software engineers were unavailable to the post-sales support group when the customer was angry about the poorly functioning product.

Despite all, this organization threw the best parties. Friday beer bashes were regular events, and the Christmas party included a lavish dinner with free-flowing drinks at a luxury hotel in the heart of Silicon Valley. Fun parties, however, could not make up for daily frustration, so retention was low at this company, even for Silicon Valley.

Not surprisingly, this company couldn't sustain financial success. At first, it took advantage of a wave of high demand for its products, but soon its reputation for poor-quality products and a revolving door of employees created an opportunity for competitors to do a better job, eclipsing this company's ability to attract and retain customers. The company was sold to an offshore holding company, and the product line was quietly assumed into other applications.

When I talk about tools, I mean any tools needed to get the job done, including both low-technology tools such as hammers and high-technology tools such as computers and devices, as well as software applications. The quality and usefulness of company-provided tools are indicative of the culture of the company.

One company used to operate a "trickle down" method of allocating new computers to employees. The salespeople and product engineers got new models every three years, while the rest of the company got "upgraded" to the sales and engineering's second-hand computers. This type of hierarchical approach to hardware allocation, or any other allocation, seldom works to create a cohesive company culture. Instead, it pits departments against each other and creates resentment among the poorly treated employees, which is exactly what happened at this company. When I pointed this out to them, they changed the policy and provided efficient hardware for all employees.

There are many proven methodologies that provide a framework for operational processes, depending on the company's industry. For example,

Lean Six Sigma is an effective methodology for manufacturing organizations and departments that produce a product, including Information Technology (IT) departments. IT departments might also follow the Information Technology Infrastructure Library (ITIL) framework to organize their processes. Agile methodology is commonly used with software engineering. Certifications of operational excellence such as ISO, the Malcolm Baldrige award, and others are beneficial in providing structure for high-quality internal processes.

Whether you use a process methodology or not, one technique that is perennially useful is to flowchart your departmental process, using sticky notes on a wall for visual impact. To do so, gather a small taskforce of experts in whatever process you plan to tackle—e.g., it could be a sales process, provisioning, or customer service—and start with a discussion of the values the taskforce wishes to embed in this process.

Using Brio Leadership's core values of excellence, (compassion, balance, integrity, and serving the world), a taskforce might decide that their intra-departmental processes will be designed to uphold the values of excellence, compassion, and integrity.

Excellence will be served by the outputs of the process, which will be of highest possible quality. Compassion will be modeled by considering the needs of everyone involved in performing job-related tasks, as well as the receivers of the team's work, including customers and other employees.

Integrity will be built into the process by defining the right thing to do, holding each team member accountable to the standards of the process, and being honest when making a mistake. Again, if you wish to embed your culture, you must refer to the core values in everything you do. The taskforce might complete a form like this:

Values the process supports:	Actions that support it:
Excellence	The outputs and results will be of highest possible quality.
Compassion	We consider the needs of each team member in performing the tasks. We consider the needs of the recipients of our work, both customers and other internal departments. We work together respectfully and lovingly.
Integrity	We do the right things and hold each team member accountable to the standards defined in this process. We do what we commit to

	doing. We admit when we make a mistake.

Next, it is important to quickly review flowcharting basics with the team. You can use the following shapes in your chart:

The ellipse represents the beginning and end of the process. Place sticky notes with this shape and Start or End drawn on them. Put them at the far left and far right side of the wall.

The rectangle represents a task or action. Most of your flowchart will be composed of rectangles. Write short task descriptions on sticky notes and order them from left to right. This will evoke interesting discussions, as it is probable that team members will disagree on the tasks and their sequence.

The diamond shape represents a decision point in the process or a metaphoric fork in the road. It is expressed as a question and has two or more flows out of the diamond, depending on the answer. Draw a diamond on a sticky note and pose a question, such as "Does this request need approval from VP?" The two paths leading out from the diamond are labeled "Yes" and "No," thus documenting the two branches of the process flow.

Operational Processes and Tools

Workflow chart for a call center operation

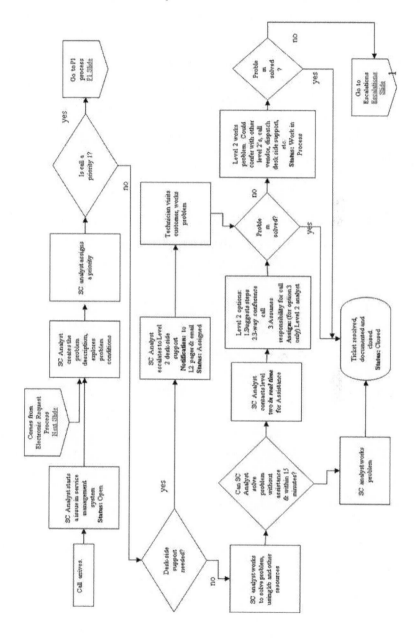

To comply with ISO and other quality certifications, the next step is to document each task identified in your flowchart. ISO protocol identifies these documents as work instructions and provides a document structure, including version control numbers, dates, and a history of who updated it.

Unless you need to follow a certification methodology, work instructions needn't be rigid or constricting but should be created in the spirit of providing guidance to all employees. For many departments, process documentation becomes a de facto knowledgebase that any employee can refer to when they are unsure how to perform a task. For this reason, your process documentation should be stored on a network drive or a database for everyone to access. If possible, the repository for written procedures should be both searchable and organized into a menu or Table of Contents structure. If, for instance, Susan doesn't even know the words to use to describe the process she needs to learn, she might want to browse the Table of Contents for what is available. However, if Susan knows exactly what she's looking for, a search of any kind is the most efficient means.

Keeping Process Documentation Up to Date

Schedule a periodic review of procedures. There are multiple tactics to keep your process documentation up to date and dynamic. One way is to encourage all employees to update documentation as they use it. If they find a better way, ask them to document the process themselves. If you have version control in your documentation, then nothing is lost. The next person can revert to the previous version or add some conditional statement to the instructions that demonstrates when to use one method over the other.

Some companies schedule a periodic review of procedures. For example, Alkali Insurance holds a process review day annually, called the "Creative Destruction Day." In that exercise, each team lists what has worked and what hasn't, and then flowcharts their processes to streamline and revise them for greater efficiency. These are lively sessions, with much disagreement among team members, but the results are updated process documents that reflect the group's best ideas at the time. This perfectly illustrates a healthy attitude toward operational processes: they are great to have but always in a state of flux, able to be honed with the input of additional experience and new ideas.

When your group, like at Alkali, discovers multiple ways to achieve the same step in the process, how do you decide which one to sanction in your documentation? The simplest and quickest method is usually the best.

What sequence of steps will get you to the desired outcome in the least amount of time and the least amount of effort? That is the best process to recommend to employees.

Interdepartmental Interfaces

Once you have all your departmental processes flowcharted and documented, it is vital to take your process mapping to the next step. This critical step is to identify how work gets transferred from one department to another.

The inability to define this hand-off causes companies untold grief, low productivity, high levels of rework, and poor internal employee relations. I had a boss who often said, "Good fences make good neighbors." What he meant by that is that if the boundaries between what one group is responsible for (and what the neighbor, or an interfacing department of the company, is responsible for), then neighbors will live harmoniously. Take this to heart and create well-defined boundaries among your departments.

In the Information Technology world, the document that outlines inter-departmental interfaces is called an Operating Level Agreement or OLA. Whatever you call it, create a document and a flowchart that defines the following elements between all the departments that work together:

- What are the outputs from one group that will be received as input in another department? How will that happen? For example, when a deal is completed in the sales department, the prospect becomes a customer. How will the accounting department invoice the customer and collect payment? How will the customer receive the product and its service?

- What information needs to be passed from the sales department to the accounting, shipping, and service departments so a seamless transition can be made?

- Remember that your customer doesn't care about inter-departmental politics or poor communication in your company. They view your company as a monolithic entity and expect the right hand to know what the left hand has done—in other words, they expect seamless service and exquisite communication from the company.

- What are the standards for acceptable outputs from one department as they become inputs to another? Going back to the new sale example, specifically what information does accounting need to receive from sales to invoice the new customer?

- Forms are usually created, either in paper or electronic form, that specify this information. Ensure that the form includes all the necessary information for accounting to complete their work. This is ideally created because of a dialogue between the sales and accounting departments.

- What are the expected response and resolution times? In our sales example, this means how soon must the accounting department acknowledge receipt (response time) of the sales order and how quickly should they invoice the customer (resolution time)? What if it's an urgent order and needs to be done more quickly than usual?

- How will the two departments communicate? Plan for periodic meetings to review process flow and work in progress, and to iron out any difficulties discovered orders. Consider also guidelines for informal communication, such as phone calls and emails among individuals in the groups. Define high-level expectations of those information exchanges: such as a tone of respect, response time expectations, full disclosure of relevant information, etc.

- What reports will you create? The adage is still true: You must measure what you manage. To measure a process, you count inputs and outputs, you measure and track how long it takes to complete the work, and you have some way to measure the quality of the outputs. In our example of an accounting group invoicing after a sale is made, you might track and report the following items every month:

Accounting Report
May 2016

	Jan	Feb	Mar
# of sales received			
# of invoices sent			
Average time to invoice			
# and % of correct invoices			
Average days to collect			

- Hours of operation and staffing. Perhaps this is implicit in your environment, but as the workplace becomes increasingly globalized, the issue of work hours is increasingly important. In the spirit of building a good fence, explicitly state each group's working hours and level of staffing during those hours.

- Remedies for non-achievement of goals. Often, when one department is annoyed with another department's lack of speed or quality in performing work, the team complains to the next higher level of management.

- Instead of escalating a grievance, the two departments could agree on a remedy for a breach of response and resolution goals (for example) that is self-efficacious. In other words, could the two groups agree that if a deadline is missed in one group, certain specified things will happen?

- For instance, if a deadline is missed in the accounting group, they will call the customer to apologize and inform the sales team of the mistake.

- Tasks each will perform (boundaries)

- Communications (meetings, informal means)

- Reporting expectations (type, frequency, roles of recipients...)

- Commitments to share knowledge

Tools List

Every company needs to provide a minimum of computer systems to its employees. The following is not meant to be an exhaustive list, but rather a suggestive one from which to pick and choose those that are relevant to your business:

- Computer systems
- Accounting, Enterprise Resource Management (ERP), Customer Relationship Management (CRM)
- Microsoft Office or equivalent
- Email/calendaring/task management system
- Knowledge database
- Customer feedback survey mechanism
- Telephone systems
- PBX or web-based system
- Automatic call distribution systems for customer service functions
- Mobile phones

Key Concepts

1. To embed your company culture into operational processes, identify the specific core value(s) each workflow upholds.

2. There are process methodologies that can help your specific business or department improve its productivity. Choose one that is best for your unique needs.

3. Any process can be improved by creating and examining a workflow chart. The best companies review this at least yearly and seek input for improvements.

4. It is counterproductive to try to build a performance-enhancing culture without providing the best work tools to employees. Ensure that the tools used are the most up-to-date and effective that you can afford and appropriate for their purposes in reinforcing a positive company culture.

CHAPTER 9

Accountability Systems

In the *Company Culture Ecosystem*, an emphasis is placed on results. If a company is not able to operate profitably, it will ultimately go out of business.

Building a great culture will not ensure profitability unless you incorporate ways to hold people accountable to the goals and standards that you have set. A great culture will help you attain higher profits only if you have the fortitude to create accountability systems into your processes.

How core values inform strategic plans and goals

Accountability is like a well-built skyscraper. Its foundations are the core values of the organization, upon which you construct the strategic vision, goals, and metrics for the organization.

Then you cascade the goals down through the organization, like a tiered fountain: to business units, departments, teams, and individuals. This ensures that every employee has a metric to meet and understands how their work contributes to the organization's success. The core values inform and direct each aspect of the accountability structure.

Strategic Plan

Every company and every department within a larger company should have a strategic plan. Ideally, the plan should look out ten years into the future; however, many of the companies I work with today balk at a ten-year window. They cite the rapid rate of change in today's business world and insist that a maximum of three years is reasonable. The best way to approach this is to create a vision for ten years into the future but make business plans in three-year increments.

The strategic plan should include the following elements:

- A current situation analysis of the company or department, including its strengths, weakness, opportunities, and threats (a SWOT analysis)

- A projection of market conditions and how they might affect the company

There are many resources to help you devise a strategic plan. Jim Horan's One-Page Business Plan (2012) and template are a great way to get started. In this method, the process of creating a business plan is streamlined so that your wishes are expressed in a one-page format. This is like the business plan proposed in the Gino Wickman's book, *Traction* (2011), and its Vision/Traction Organizer template. A third option is Verne Harnish's *One Page Strategic Plan* (2014). Any of these resources can help you develop a strategic plan that is based on the core values of your company. To repeat, the helpful instructions found in these books is outside the scope of this volume, but we'll highlight a few key concepts.

At Brio Leadership, we approach strategy through three lenses: the compass, the filter, and the map. You can download our Simple Strategic Plan on Brio Leadership's website at www.brioleadership.com/resources.

First, the compass represents the set of guiding principles by which you conduct business. It includes your core values and purpose statement.

This filter defines what customers, problems, and solutions you will and will not pursue. Often, identifying the market segment to which you do not wish to market yourself is the most beneficial discernment you can make because it keeps you focused on your ideal customer.

At Brio Leadership, we approach strategy through three lenses: the compass, the filter, and the map.

Lastly, the map defines how you will be successful over time, including three-year and one-year goals and objectives.

Your culture, the industry, and the size of your company will determine how many fewer people to include in the planning process that devises the strategic plan. Some companies include only their top leadership team (the C suite) in this exercise; others involve a task force with representatives from all departments. Usually companies host a facilitated off-site meeting to create a strategic plan. At the off-site meeting, the team decides on the outline of the plan and delegates the actual writing of the plan.

Once you have created an initial plan, updating it every year will become easier, and your leadership team can spend less time shaping the plan for the coming year.

Annual Goals and the Balanced Scorecard

For annual goals, it is important to restrict the number of goals to the three or four most important ones, excluding your revenue goal. Chris McChesney calls these "Wildly Important Goals" or WIGs (McChesney 2012, 10), and James Collins calls them a "Big Hairy Audacious Goal" or BHAG (Collins 2001).

A Balanced Scorecard

In our experience, companies that have only a revenue goal for the year typically meet their goal while sacrificing everything else. One company we worked with focused maniacally on their revenue goal for a year. They achieved their goal and threw a lavish party in celebration of their accomplishment. However, the next year the company failed to reach even the previous year's historic revenue level, let alone the new annual goal, because they had grown revenues without increasing the internal capabilities of the company. For that reason, it is important that you select goals that are well-balanced and mindful of the holistic health of the company.

One paradigm that helps leaders consider a balanced array of goals is called the Balanced Scorecard (Kaplan and Norton 1996, 9) which identifies four areas or perspectives that a company must manage and measure: Financial; Internal Business Process; Learning and Growth; and Customer.

The meaning of the financial perspective is self-evident and includes metrics such as revenue, profit margin, and expenses.

The internal business process perspective focuses on metrics concerning any initiative from the Operational Processes and Tools element of the *Company Culture Ecosystem*. This would include implementation of new enterprise tools, such as a CRM or ERP system, or process improvements like completing ISO documentation or implementation of Agile software development methodology.

The Learning and Growth perspective is directed toward employee and organizational learning and measures achievements such as individual and site certifications, internal promotions; employee satisfaction, and retention rates. The Customer perspective measures goal achievement in areas of product innovation, customer service and loyalty, and brand awareness.

When choosing three or four important annual goals for your company, use the Balanced Scorecard as a template for goals that represent all the important perspectives of your company.

Cascading Goals

Too many companies spend a lot of time and money on a strategic plan and stop there. They put the plan on a shelf and refer to it only in quarterly meetings. However, to keep strategy alive, a good technique is to "cascade" the plan down through the organization.

The term cascading conjures up an image of a fancy party with a chocolate fountain into which guests can dip strawberries. The chocolate starts at the top and cascades down the fountain into increasingly larger levels. Likewise, cascading a strategic plan ensures that you start at the top with a company plan and then propagate elements of the plan throughout the organization to increasingly larger groups of team members, from business units to departments and ultimately to the individual employees.

The way to accomplish this is to ask all the business units and departments to develop three to four annual goals that support the over-arching company goals. They might consider having their own off-site meetings with their leadership teams to develop the year's goals. Then, ask each manager to work with their team members to develop individual goals and metrics for the year and include them in their performance evaluation.

Be sure that every individual in the company has at least one "number" to achieve that will advance the company's goals. For example, even a receptionist can influence the customer's loyalty, and you can measure that with a customer survey that includes a question about their impression of the company when visiting or calling it.

Cascade goals like a chocolate fountain

Give the receptionist a goal that is within his control and hold him accountable to it.

When you present the annual goals, be sure to also present the core values they represent. If you don't use a one-page format that already includes values, such as those mentioned above, create your own format so each goal is visually mapped back to the core value it supports.

Here is an example of cascading goals for a customer service department:

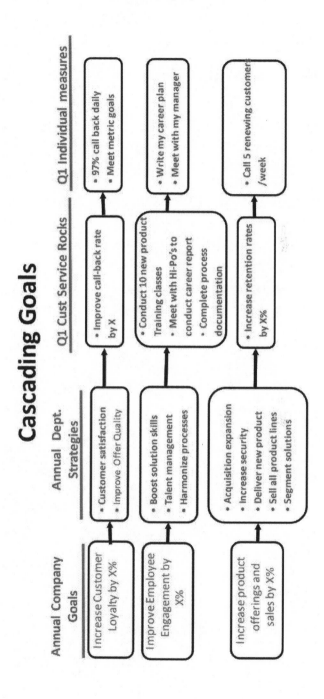

Cascading Goals

Annual Company Goals | **Annual Dept. Strategies** | **Q1 Cust Service Rocks** | **Q1 Individual measures**

Increase Customer Loyalty by X%
- Customer satisfaction
- Improve Offer Quality
- Improve call-back rate by X
- 97% call back daily
- Meet metric goals

Improve Employee Engagement by X%
- Boost solution skills
- Talent management
- Harmonize processes
- Conduct 10 new product Training classes
- Meet with Hi-Po's to conduct career report
- Complete process documentation
- Write my career plan
- Meet with my manager

Increase product offerings and sales by X%
- Acquisition expansion
- Increase security
- Deliver new product
- Sell all product lines
- Segment solutions
- Increase retention rates by X%
- Call 5 renewing customers /week

Leading and Lagging Measures

It is important to understand the difference between leading and lagging measures as you define metrics for your company, departments, and individuals. Here is a succinct definition:

- **Leading measures** track activities that are necessary to produce results. They are measures of tasks and events and are therefore relatively easy to measure. Some examples include sales calls made by salesperson, service calls received, and the number of widgets produced in a manufacturing facility.

- **Lagging measures** track results or outcomes of the leading activities and align to business goals. They are often harder to measure and

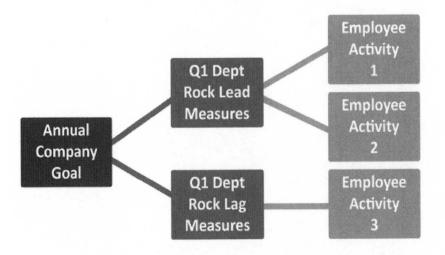

include metrics such as company profit, customer loyalty, and employee retention.

If we remember that lagging measures track the results of activities done in your company, most of your company's objectives should be lagging measures and most individual goals should be leading measures. Departmental goals can be a mixture of leading and lagging measures.

Within this paradigm, an example of a company's three most important annual goals (and the core value it upholds) could be:

Leading and lagging measures

Annual Goal—Company:	Value(s) it supports:
Release the XYZ product by year end	Excellence
Retain ninety two percent of existing customers	Customer service
Attain ISO certification	Excellence, Customer service, Continual learning

Notice that these goals are lagging measures, which are the result of activities done within the company. Notice also that the goals do not include financial goals but align with the Customer and Internal Business Process perspectives of the Balanced Scorecard. The financial goal for the year would be included on the one-page business plan.

An example of a department's goals might be:

Annual goals—Department X:	Value(s) it supports:
Increase retention rates by 1 percent	Excellence, Customer service
Identify 10 percent of mission-critical defects in the new product	Excellence, Customer service
Document all departmental processes	Excellence, Customer service, Continual learning, Respect

Notice again that only one of these annual goals is a lagging measure (the first one), and all others are leading measures. Increasing retention rates is a result of many activities you do, so it is a lagging measure. The rest of the goals in the example are activities. The departmental goals can be a mixture.

Generally, individual goals are leading measures. A salesperson in your company might have the following goals that support those of the company. Notice that these are leading measures at the individual level.

Annual goals— Salesperson Y:	Value(s) it supports:
Call five existing customers every week to assess their satisfaction	Excellence, Customer service
Make $X in new sales	Excellence
Call ten prospective clients every week	Excellence, Customer service

Metrics and Reporting

As noted previously, the discipline of cascading annual goals down to the individual ensures that (1) all employees are aware of the company's goals and direction for the year and (2) everyone understands how they can contribute to achieving the company's goal. This practice creates alignment and transparency between leaders and employees. If used with the performance evaluation practices discussed in the chapter on People Practices, it will enhance the effectiveness and productivity of your company.

Another step in completing this process is to monitor progress toward the goals. It is counterproductive to give everyone a number to achieve for the year and then not report and monitor at least monthly efforts toward the goal. It makes sense to report metrics at all levels to which the goals were cascaded from company, to business unit, to department, and to individual.

It is important that metrics be tied into a performance evaluation and variable pay formulas. In that way, you ensure focus on the metrics. Just be sure the metrics are fair, attainable, and tied to the core values of the company. Here is a scorecard template for reporting:

2016 GOALS/METRICS	Q1 Targets	Jan	Feb	Mar	Q2 Targets	April	May	Jun	Q3 Targets	Etc.
1.										
2.										
3.										

Department Scorecard: 2016

Meetings to Track Progress toward Goals

As noted in the chapter on rituals, meetings are one of management's primary rituals. To use meeting time wisely is the trick.

Here is a cadence of meetings that make sense to many companies:

The Daily Team Huddle

This is a standing meeting that makes sense for smaller groups that need to coordinate efforts on a frequent basis. This type of meeting is recommended in both Agile development methodology and in Rockefeller Habits (Harnish 178–183). Note the unique characteristics of the Daily Team Huddle:

- It lasts no longer than fifteen minutes

- The team meets standing up (in a huddle), not seated at a table.

- Each attendee reports answers to three simple questions:

  1. What did I accomplish yesterday?

  2. What will I do today?

  3. Here's where I'm stuck and need help.

Here is an example of a Morning Report that you could review in the Huddle. It's short and sweet:

Morning Report: September 27, 2016

	Yesterday:	MTD:	YTD:
Leads offered:			
Response emails sent:			
Outbound calls made:			
Sales closed:			

I've seen instances in which the Daily Huddle did *not* work for one team member: He was in Texas, while the rest of the team was in California. While the Californians met at 8:00 Pacific time, the meeting occurred in the middle of the Texan's morning, at 10:00 Central Time. He was working alone on website projects, while the rest of the team was enhancing a CRM system. There was no interface, or even overlap of expertise, between the differing projects. To make matters worse, the meetings droned on for thirty to forty minutes. This young engineer saw the Huddle as a waste of his time and excused himself from the meeting.

This story illustrates several important caveats about the Huddle: The entire team must be working on the same or similar projects so they can offer help to each other, and the meeting must be held at a convenient time for all, preferably at the beginning of the workday. Furthermore, it doesn't do anyone any good to force attendance on people who cannot benefit from the time spent. Lastly, it is important that the fifteen-minute meeting duration is strictly enforced.

Every day across the globe, too many workers waste time in poorly conceived meetings. It is important that you use meeting time as the precious commodity it is.

Meeting Cadence

In addition to the Daily Huddle, you might consider creating this cadence of meetings:

- Weekly Team meetings
- Quarterly Leadership meetings
- Annual planning meetings

In the chapter on rituals, we introduced a spreadsheet for meeting planning. Be sure to map each meeting to a core value, so you will be embedding your culture at every chance.

Key Concepts

1. Values form the basis for your strategic plan, which should map out where the company is headed, what customers it will attract, and one-year goals.

2. Cascading goals down through the organization ensure that everyone in the company has a number to achieve.

3. Plan your meeting cadence to embed cultural values and ensure communication.

Sidebar Conversation: Envisioning Goals

One interesting ritual I found in two of the companies I observed was the annual creation of vision boards (also called photo maps or treasure boards) by each team

member. A vision board is a visual representation, using pictures cut from magazines and glued to a poster board, of the personal goals you have for the coming year.

I have done a personal vision board for years, but not in a corporate setting. I was intrigued at first and then became convinced this is a great ritual for both team building and for connecting team members' personal goals to their work at your company. And, if you have a corporate goal of Putting Employees First or Respect for Employees, this is an effective way to embed that value into the culture.

Both companies that I studied hold special meetings during January for their team members to create their own photomaps.

At Marketwave, a marketing agency, CEO Tina Young explains the process: "I instruct each person to come up with a goal for the various areas of their lives, using the acronym RICHES For LIFE, which stands for

A photomap

Relationships, Intellect, Contribution, Home, Economy & Finance, Spirituality, Fitness & Health, and Leisure. I invite them to find a visual from a magazine that represents each of their goals. Everyone brings in magazines from home in January. We gather around the big table and devote two hours to create the photomaps."

The company provides each employee with a photo frame (eleven-by-fourteen inches in size) and asks each team member to display their vision boards on their desks or bulletin boards.

At Acuity Systems, CEO Tom Niesen also has a company-wide vision board ritual. One of his team member's vision board is pictured at the top of this article.

Tom encourages them to mark off the goals as they are completed during the year. If you examine the vision boards at the top of the article, you might notice the word "DONE" marked across two of the photos.

Tom wants to help his team members achieve their personal goals. He explains it by saying,

"You will see a treasure board on our people's walls with pictures of what they want to get, accomplish, or buy next year. Once we figure out what they want to accomplish, we say, 'What can we do to help you get that house, and how much work do we do to accomplish it?' We take the big picture and break it into our rocks or quarterly goals for the year."

How to Create a Photomap

Here is a list of the materials you need to hold a vision boards meeting at your company:

Poster boards for each team member (Marketwave uses boards measuring eight × ten inches, while Acuity Systems and I use boards measuring twenty-two by fourteen inches [half of a standard poster board].)

Lots of colorful magazines or a computer and a color printer

Scissors or a paper cutter

Glue sticks

A recommendation of the major life areas to be included in the photomap

Optional: snacks to eat during the meeting

Optional: a picture frame for each team member

I recommend setting aside two hours as a company or as a department to create these vision boards. This can become an annual ritual at your company, and one that team members will look forward to. Note, however, that it can take up to a week for team members to complete their vision boards. It took me five days to finish mine because I kept thinking of new items to include or better ways to depict my goals. You can let team members take home their poster board and pictures to do the final gluing on their own time.

At your company's next departmental meetings, encourage team members to present and explain their vision boards. Then ask how the rest of the team can support each other in attaining their goals. Additionally, at the next one-on-one meeting between the team member and her manager, the manager should offer support in achieving the team member's goals for the next year. Lastly, ask each person to display their vision boards at their desk or on their bulletin board so it is always visible.

I highly recommend this practice to:

Connect employee's personal goals to their work at your company

To have a meaningful and fun New Year ritual and

Build teamwork as the teams create and support each other to achieve their dreams.

Afterward

There is no doubt that company culture is important to any size company and it is worth investing time and a little money in creating a positive one. Knowing now that you can simply change the way you do the things you already do demystifies culture and allows a holistic view of culture. *The Company Culture Ecosystem* provides a context to see your culture in a new light.

There are several takeaway concepts I'd like to leave with you:

- Culture is not just throwing good parties. Rather, it is the result of everything you do in your organization, from operational processes, how you hold people accountable, and all aspects of people management.

- Creating values and a purpose statement is a worthless endeavor unless you work to embed them into everything you do.

- Explicitly identify the values you wish to uphold in activities as diverse as strategic plans, people programs, operational processes, and leadership development programs.

- Invest in your leaders and their development. The quickest way to change a culture for the better is to change the way leaders lead. Have zero-tolerance for leadership behaviors that are non-compliant with core values, even if the leader is otherwise effective in her role.

- Food is a powerful symbol of a company culture. Devise food rituals that reflect the values of the company and use them wisely to embody the positive aspects of your culture. Remember to capitalize on the fact that serving food represents nurturing and warmth to people.

Of all things, remember that culture is what you do daily. As Will Durant said, "We are what we repeatedly do. Excellence, then, is not an act, but a habit." Culture, like excellence, must become a habit that is embedded by repetitive, daily action. Examine your daily habits and you will uncover your culture.

References

Backman, Melvin. 2014. "Best Companies to Work For" have the Best Performing Stocks. Money.cnn.com. http://money.cnn.com/2014/08/13/investing/good-workplace-stocks/.

Baker, Tim. 2013. The End of the Performance Review: A New Approach to Appraising Employee Performance. New York: Palgrave Macmillan.

Beck, Don, and Christopher Cowan. 1996. *Spiral Dynamics: Mastering Values, Leadership and Change.* Malden, MA: Blackwell Publishing.

Barrett, Richard. 1998. *Liberating the Corporate Soul: Building a Visionary Organization.* Woburn, MA: Butterworth-Heinemann.

Barrett, Richard. 2014. "Building Trust in Your Team: The Trust Matrix." https://richardbarrettblog.net/2014/04/11/building-trust-in-your-team-the-trust-matrix/

Bass, Bernard M. 1985. *Leadership and Performance Beyond Expectations.* New York: The Free Press.

Cabral-Cardoso, Carlos, and Miguel. P. E Cunha. (2003). "The Business Lunch: Toward a Research Agenda." *Leadership & Organization Development Journal* 24 (7/8): 371–79.

Collins, Jim. 2001. *Good to Great.* New York: Harper Collins.

Deal, Terry, and Allan Kennedy. 2000. *Corporate Cultures: The Rites and Rituals of Corporate Life* (1st ed.). Cambridge, Mass: Basic Books.

Denison, Daniel R. 1984. "Bringing Corporate Culture to the Bottom Line." *Organizational Dynamics* 13 (2): 5–22. Retrieved from http://www.denisonconsulting.com/sites/defau lt/files/documents/resources/denison-1984-culture-bottom-line_0.pdf.

Driver, Michaela. 2008. "Every Bite You Take...Food and the Struggles of Embodied Subjectivity in Organizations." *Human Relations* 61 (7): 913–34. http://doi.org/10.1177/0018726708093902.

Fischler, Claude. 2011. "Commensality, Society and Culture." *Social Science Information* 50 (3–4): 528–48.

Goleman, Daniel, Richard Boyatzis, and Annie McKee. (2002). *Primal Leadership: Realizing the Power of Emotional Intelligence.* Boston, MA: Harvard Business School Press.

Gottman, John. 2001. The Relationship Cure: A 5 Step Guide to Strengthening Your Marriage, Family, and Friendships. New York: Three Rivers Press.

Greenleaf, Robert. 2002. *Servant Leadership: A Journey into the Nature of Legitimate Power and Greatness.* New Jersey: Paulist Press.

Harnish, Verne. 2014. *Scaling Up: How a Few Companies Make it...and Why the Rest Don't.* Ashburn, VA: Gazelles, Inc.

Higginbottom, Karen. "Bad Bosses at the Heart of Employee Turnover" in *Forbes* http://www.forbes.com/sites/karenhigginbotto m/2015/09/08/bad-bosses-at-the-heart-of-employee-turnover/#30c93d7a4075.

Hildebrandt, Terry, and Kent Webb. 2016. "How Providers become Leaders: Coaching Healthcare Providers and Leaders to be Great People Leaders," in *Choice Magazine*, v. 4 #2.

Horan, Jim. 2012. *The One Page Business Plan: Start with a Business, Build a Company!* Berkeley, CA: The One Page Business Plan Company.

Joiner, Bill, and Stephen Josephs. 2007. *Leadership Agility: Five Levels of Mastery for Anticipating and Initiating Change.* San Francisco: Jossey-Bass.

Julier, Alice P. 2013. *Eating Together: Food, Friendship and Inequality* (1st ed.). Urbana: University of Illinois Press.

Jung, Tobias, Tim Scott, Huw T. O. Davies, Peter Bower, Diane Whalley, Rosalind McNally, and Russell Mannion. 2009. "Instruments for

Exploring Organizational Culture: A Review of the Literature." *Public Administration Review* 69 (6): 1087–96.

Kaplan, Robert S., and David P. Norton. 1996. *The Balanced Scorecard: Translating Strategy into Action.* Boston: Harvard Business School Press.

Kemp, Linzi J., and Paul Williams. 2013. "In Their Own Time and Space: Meeting Behaviour in the Gulf Arab Workplace." *International Journal of Cross Cultural Management* 13 (2): 215–35.

Kimsey-House, Henry, Karen Kimsey-House, Phillip Sandahl, and Laura Whitworth. 2011. *Co-Active Coaching: Changing Business, Transforming Lives.* 3rd ed. Boston: Nicholas Brealy Publishing.

Keyton, Joann. 2011. Communication and Organizational Culture: A Key to Understanding Work Experiences. Thousand Oaks, A: Sage Publications.

Kotter, John P., and James. L Heskett. 1992. *Corporate Culture and Performance.* New York: Free Press.

Levenson, Robert W., Paul Ekman, and Matthieu Ricard. 2016. "Meditation and the Startle Response: A Case Study." *Emotion* (Washington, D.C.) 12.3 (2012): 650–58. PMC. Web. 9.

Lisita, Ellie. 2012. *The Positive Perspective: Dr. Gottman's Magic Ratio!*

https://www.gottman.com/blog/the-positive-perspective-dr-gottmans-magic-ratio/

MacGregor, Douglas. 2006. The Human Side of Enterprise, Annotated Edition. McGraw-Hill Education, Print.

MacLean, Anna Kaye. 2013. Facebook post. https://www.facebook.com/photo.php?fbid=4767574347510&set=o.106027143213&type=1&theater

Mackey, John, Rajendra Sisodia, and Bill George. 2014. *Conscious Capitalism: Liberating the Heroic Spirit of Business* (2nd ed.). Boston, Massachusetts: Harvard Business Review Press.

McChesney, Chris, Sean Covey, and Jim Huling. 2012. *The 4 Disciplines of Execution: Achieving your Wildly Important Goals.* New York: Free Press.

Miller, Lisa, Paul Rozin, and Alan P. Fiske. 1998. "Food Sharing and Feeding another Person Suggest Intimacy; Two Studies of American College Students." *Eur. J. Soc. Psychol.,* 28: 423–36. doi: 10.1002/(SICI)1099-0992(199805/06)28:3<423: AID-EJSP874>3.0.CO;2-V

Peters, Tom J., and Robert H. Waterman, Jr. (2006). *In Search of Excellence: Lessons from America's*

Best-Run Companies (Reprint ed.). New York: HarperBusiness.

Plester, Barbara. 2014. "Ingesting the Organization: The Embodiment of Organizational Food Rituals." *Culture and Organization* 21 (3): 251–68. http://doi.org/10.1080/14759551.2013.873798

Rhoades, Ann., Stephen. R Covey, and Nancy Shepherdson. 2011. *Built on Values: Creating an Enviable Culture that Outperforms the Competition* (1st ed.). San Francisco: Jossey-Bass.

Schein, Edgar H. 2010. *Organizational Culture and Leadership* (4th ed.). San Francisco, Calif: Jossey-Bass.

Sisodia, Rajendra, Jagdish N. Sheth, and David B. Wolfe. 2014. *Firms of Endearment: How World-Class Companies Profit from Passion and Purpose* (2nd ed.). Upper Saddle River, New Jersey: Pearson FT Press.

Smith, Aaron. C. T., and Bob Stewart. 2011. "Organizational Rituals: Features, Functions and Mechanisms." *International Journal of Management Reviews* 13 (2): 113–33. http://doi.org/10.1111/j.1468-2370.2010.00288.x.

Sørensen, Jesper B. 2002. "The Strength of Corporate Culture and the Reliability of Firm

Performance." *Administrative Science Quarterly* 47 (1): 70–91. http://doi.org/10.2307/3094891.

Spiegelman, Paul. 2012, April 17. Why Every Company Needs a Culture Chief. *Inc.com.* http://www.inc.com/paul-spiegelman/why-every-company-needs-a-culture-chief.html.

Thomson, Di, and Anne-Marie Hassenkamp. 2008. "The Social Meaning and Function of Food Rituals in Healthcare Practice: An Ethnography." *Human Relations* 61 (12): 1775–802.

Torbert, William R., and Susanne R. Cook-Greuter. 2004. *Action inquiry: the secret of timely and transforming leadership.* San Francisco, CA: Berrett-Koehler. http://www.aspresolver.com/aspresolver.asp?B IZP;2360028

Trice, Harrison, and Janice M. Beyer. 1984. "Studying Organizational Cultures though Rites and Ceremonials." *Academy of Management Review* 9 (4): 653–69. http://doi.org/10.5465/AMR.1984.4277391.

Valentine, Gill. 2002. "In-Corporations: Food, Bodies and Organizations." *Body & Society* 8 (2): 1–20. http://doi.org/10.1177/1357034X0200800200 1.

Wickman, Gino. 2012. *Traction: Get a Grip on Your Business.* New York: BenBella Books, Inc.

http://public.eblib.com/choice/publicfullrecord.
aspx?p=900253.

Wigglesworth, Cindy. 2012. *SQ21: The Twenty-One Skills of Spiritual Intelligence.* New York: Select Books.

About Kristin Robertson

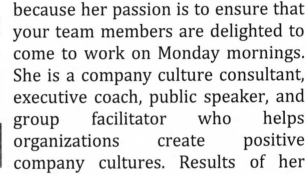Kristin Robertson is the Happy Mondays Coach, because her passion is to ensure that your team members are delighted to come to work on Monday mornings. She is a company culture consultant, executive coach, public speaker, and group facilitator who helps organizations create positive company cultures. Results of her work include reduced operational costs, high-performing employees, productive teams, and articulated strategic goals. As an executive coach, Robertson works with executives and high-potential managers to increase their self-awareness and leadership effectiveness. She is a skilled group facilitator who leads executive off-site meetings that increase teamwork, self-awareness, and leadership effectiveness.

Ms. Robertson is the founder and president of the Company Culture Consortium of Dallas (www.companycultureconsortium.com), a chapter of the Academy of Culture Ambassadors. This professional association provides opportunities for education, sharing of best practices and community building among culture experts.

Ms. Robertson is a faculty member at the University of Texas at Dallas' Executive Education department, where she facilitates leadership workshops. She is President-Elect of the International Coach Federation (ICF) North-Texas chapter, and holds the second-highest credential from the ICF, called Professional Certified Coach. She recently completed a second master's degree in Organizational Development and Leadership and a certificate in Evidence-Based Coaching from Fielding Graduate University.

Her clients include Schneider Electric, Aflac, Hewlett-Packard, 7-Eleven, Southwest Airlines, AT&T, BMC, Texas Wesleyan University School of Health Professions, Federal Emergency Management Agency, Salmon Sims Thomas PCC, Susan B. Komen for the Cure and Texas Children's Hospital.

Before starting Brio Leadership, she was a consultant to IT help desks and high technology companies to optimize their technical support processes. She was a faculty member of the HDI (Help Desk Institute) University for six years and taught all the certification courses it offered. Kristin conducted site audits of technical support centers, comparing them to the Service Capability and Performance standards created by Service Strategies Corporation.

Kristin held executive positions including Vice President of Client Services at Advent Software in Silicon Valley, where she helped prepare the organization for its Initial Public Offering, and director at Fidelity Investments, where she won the President's Award in 1996.

Kristin trained as a classical musician in her youth and received her first master's degree from the New England Conservatory of Music in viola performance. She recently returned to playing viola after a twenty-three-year hiatus while raising her children. She now performs as principal violist of two community orchestras and plays in her church's orchestra.

Ms. Robertson lives in Dallas/Fort Worth, Texas, with her husband and Remy, a miniature poodle mix.

Need More Help?

Although this book was intended to be a guidebook for culture engineers, sometimes you need a little more help to guide you in your culture transformation. Or, your team may be too busy running the business to get the culture foundations built. In either case, we're here to help.

Happy Mondays Club Self-Study Course

Wouldn't it be great to have access to all the best practices you've discovered in this book – in a digital form that could save you hours of work? Ms. Robertson has created an online-learning course called the Happy Mondays Club, which has even more tips and tricks for establishing and maintaining a positive and productive company culture. Of most importance are forty-two downloadable templates, documents and forms that will propel your culture transformation and save you the time and effort of creating them yourself. The course offers recorded videos of Kristin leading you through ten lessons for building a great company culture. You also receive the PowerPoint slides, a podcast recording and a learner's manual. Please visit www.happymondaysclub.com for more information. Use discount code TheBook for a 10% discount off list price.

Assess Your Culture

Brio Leadership uses a scientifically-based assessment from Human Synergistics to baseline your current culture and define your ideal culture, based on feedback from your team. We can work with your leadership team to present the current situation and map your journey to your desired culture. By using a proven assessment, you can set a baseline of your culture and measure improvements you make by implementing the recommendations in this book. Visit us at www.brioleadership.com/company-culture-audit.html for more information.

Coaching is the Best Way to Change your Culture!

Both individual and group coaching have been proven to change your leader's behaviors, which is the most powerful way to change your culture. Brio Leadership provides a comprehensive package of coaching options to fit the needs of your organization. Studies have shown that the return on investment in coaching is over 600%. To learn more about our coaching options, please visit our website at www.brioleadership.com/coaching.html

Leadership Development Workshops

Brio Leadership has a full curriculum of leadership development workshops, including The Leadership Challenge curriculum from James Kouzes and Barry Posner and advanced topics such as emotional intelligence and influence. Training workshops are always followed by group or individual coaching to hold learners accountable to their action plans and to assist with changing behaviors. Whether this is part of your culture change or an initiative to train the next generation of leaders in your organization, Brio Leadership has the expertise to help you develop talent. Visit us at www.brioleadership.com/the-leadership-challenge.html.

Book Kristin as a speaker

Kristin Robertson is delighted to facilitate or present to your leadership off-site meeting, women's network, or monthly training meeting. Here is just a sampling of the topics she presents:

- Measure what Matters: How to Assess and Build a Company Culture of Accountability
- Mindful Leadership: Mindfulness Practices that Help you Become an Intentional Leader
- Spectacular Leadership Skills
- Women's Leadership Skills

Call Brio Leadership at 817-577-7030
-OR-
Visit our website at
http://www.brioleadership.com/contact.html
and complete a contact form.

Made in the USA
Lexington, KY
17 October 2019